Nestor
and the Eichenfeld Massacre

A Civil War Tragedy
in a Ukrainian Mennonite Village

This book is published as part of the

TSARIST AND SOVIET MENNONITE STUDIES SERIES

A publication series sponsored by the Research Program in Tsarist and Mennonite Studies, a program within the Centre for Russian and East European Studies, University of Toronto. The series includes research guides, source collections, and studies.

General Editor, Harvey L. Dyck
Associate Editor, John R. Staples

Nestor Makhno and the Eichenfeld Massacre

A Civil War Tragedy in a Ukrainian Mennonite Village

Compiled, Edited, Translated, and with an Introduction and Analysis by

Harvey L. Dyck, John R. Staples and John B. Toews

Published by
Pandora Press

National Library of Canada Cataloguing
in Publication data pending

NESTOR MAKHNO AND THE EICHENFELD MASSACRE: A CIVIL WAR TRAGEDY IN A UKRAINIAN MENNONITE VILLAGE
Copyright © 2004 by Pandora Press
33 Kent Avenue
Kitchener, Ontario N2G 3R2
All rights reserved.

International Standard Book Number: 1-894710-46-0

Book design: Nathan Stark
Cover Design: Christian Snyder
Cover photograph: Designed by Canadian artist Paul Epp, Eichenfeld memorial for victims of massacre on day of unveiling.

All Pandora Press books are printed on Eco-Logo certified paper.

12 11 10 09 08 07 06 05 04   12 11 10 9 8 7 6 5 4 3 2 1

IN SORROWFUL REMEMBRANCE
Mennonite Victims of Civil War
Murders and Massacres in the
Nikolaipole Volost
1918-1920
Adelsheim/Dolinovka
Eichenfeld/Dubovka (Novopetrovka)
Franzfeld/Varvarovka
Gerhardstal
Hochfeld/Morozovka
Nikolaifeld/Nikolaipole
Paulsheim
Petersdorf
"They will beat their swords into ploughshares
and their spears into pruning hooks."
Isaiah 2:4

Contents

Foreword   9

PART I: CONTEXT AND THEMES
Chapter 1   Anne Konrad, Returning to Eichenfeld, May 27, 2001   15
Chapter 2   Editors, Narrative and Analysis   25
Chapter 3   Paul Epp, The Memorial as Metaphor   42

PART II: MENNONITE WITNESSES
Chapter 4   Isaak Epp, A Time of Darkness   45
Chapter 5   David A. Quiring, Eichenfeld under the Black Cloud   53
Chapter 6   Helena Harder Martens and Katharina Harder Pätkau, A Night of Horror   67
Chapter 7   Abraham Kröker, The Tent Missionaries   72

PART III: UKRAINIAN RECOLLECTIONS
Chapter 8   Oral History Interviews Conducted Under Direction of Svetlana Bobyleva   79

PART IV: REFLECTIONS
Chapter 9   Fedor G. Turchenko, Those Evil Times   93
Chapter 10   John B. Toews, Let there be Peace   96

PART V: IN MEMORIAM

Chapter 11	Mennonite Victims of Civil War Murders and Massacres in the Nikolaipole Volost 1918-1920	105
Chapter 12	Inscription	113
Chapter 13	Memorial Program, May 27, 2001	114

Foreword
In Sorrowful Remembrance

The nighttime massacre on October 26 to 27, 1919 of 136 innocent Mennonites at Eichenfeld/Dubovka (Novopetrovka) was one of numerous atrocities of the Russian revolution and civil war in the Nikolaipole volost during the years 1918-1920. The attackers, known as Makhnovites, *Makhnovtsi* in Ukrainian, after their anarchist leader Nestor Makhno, were a large, ragtag, half-bandit, half-revolutionary mounted peasant military force. During the last months of 1919 the Makhnovites occupied a huge area along the Dnieper River including multi-village Ukrainian Mennonite settlements like the Nikolaipole volost. The victims were pacifist men, women and children, neither partisans nor combatants, but peaceful villagers and visiting evangelists. The horror and insecurity of the times did not permit the dead of Eichenfeld to be openly mourned. Unwashed, they were hastily buried in shallow graves before surviving family members and villagers fled into nearby Mennonite villages.

Eighty-two years later, on Sunday, May 27, 2001, Mennonites and Ukrainians gathered at the burial site to acknowledge the Eichenfeld massacre and to honour the memory of the dead. In an act of human solidarity, a large group of residents from the surrounding villages who were in attendance adopted the memorial as their own and promised to care for it. The gray granite slab resting on granite blocks is in the form of a traditional Mennonite coffin on trestles. It is intended symbolically to give these almost-forgotten victims the dignified public viewing they had not received and to affirm the Christian pacifist conviction that violence in human relations is ineffectual and wrong. This volume contains the story of the massacre, Mennonite eyewitness accounts of it, reminiscences of the event by Ukrainians, an analysis of its origins and roots and reflections on its legacy. As editors, our fondest hope is that the remains of the Nikolaifeld Mennonite volost victims of civil war savagery, reposing in graves under a tangled thicket of trees and bushes, may rest in peace.

The Eichenfeld village memorial and its attendant unveiling service was the first major project of the International Mennonite Memorial Committee for the Former Soviet Union, founded in 1999. From six countries on four continents, the present members of the Committee are Harvey Dyck, Co-Chair, Canada; Johannes Dyck, Örlinghausen, Germany; Paul Epp, Designer, Toronto; Gerhard Hildebrandt, Göttingen, Germany; Peter Klassen, Co-Chair, Fresno, California, USA; Boris Letkeman, Zaporizhe, Ukraine; Natasha Ostasheva, Dnepropetrovsk, Ukraine; Gerhard Ratzlaff, Asuncion, Paraguay; John R. Staples, Secretary, Fredonia, New York State, USA; John B. Toews, Vancouver, Canada; Walter Unger, Toronto, Canada; and Petr Vibe, Omsk, Russia.

Among its many supporters, the Memorial Committee would like to thank in particular the following for help in the realization of this pioneering venture: The Anabaptist Foundation Canada; Paul Epp, Toronto, who designed the monument; The Institute of Ukrainian-German Studies, directed by Svetlana Bobyleva, National University of Dnepropetrovsk, Ukraine; Liudmila Kariaka, Olga Shmakina and Larissa Goryacheva, Intourist, Zaporizhe; Mennonite Central Committee, Akron, Pennsylvania; Mennonite Centre Ukraine, Molochansk, Ukraine; Boris Letkeman, Chair, Board of the Zaporizhe Mennonite church; Aleksandr Pankeev and his daughter, Zaporizhe, master stone-masons who produced the memorial; The Centre for Russian and East European Studies, University of Toronto, which organized the project; Mikhail M. Sidorenko, Executive Director, Zaporizhe Oblast Committee for the Protection and Preservation of Historical Monuments; Aleksandr Tedeev, Director, Regional State Archive of Zaporizhe; Fedor Turchenko, Chair, History, State University of Zaporizhe, Ukraine; and the village council (*selsovet*) of Novopetrovka.

We are grateful to relatives of the victims who, with friends of the Mennonite story around the world, generously covered the direct costs of the project.

PART I
CONTEXT AND THEMES

Chapter 1
Returning to Eichenfeld, May 27, 2001

Anne Konrad, Journal

Today the Intourist bus is filled with friends and relatives and descendants of victims of the infamous Eichenfeld massacre. From the hotel we set out early on this bright Sunday morning in high anticipation. It feels like a class outing. The morning itinerary includes the one-time Mennonite villages of Petersdorf, Reinfeld, Franzfeld and Hochfeld, all in the Nikolaipol/Iazikova "estate area" where the Peters, Regehr and Siemens' family members on our bus are looking for a house, a school, a cemetery, something left by their parents, grandparents or other relatives connected with the Eichenfeld massacre.

Briefly the bus halts at the city market where our guide Olga Shmakina and project coordinator Harvey Dyck purchase a blue plastic pail of pink peonies. You need flowers to grace a memorial. In the deserted square a lone Communist protester sits beside a record player blaring out the International. As we leave Zaporozhe, once the centre of Mennonite life in then-Aleksandrovsk, we proceed along broad Lenin Boulevard, pass the colossal statue of Lenin, his outstretched hand seemingly forever pointing to the Dnieper River and mighty Dneprostroi dam, and cross a bridge. A large lake was created here by the flooding for Stalin's massive power plant built in the early 1930s. "They say you can still see old Einlage Mennonite houses and graves down there, but the people were relocated."

Rolling through spring green countryside we look for signs, vestiges of earlier Mennonite homes, villages or estates. "This is it! This is it!" Anita Toews calls out. She and her husband from Ann Arbor, Michigan along with her eighty-year-old mother Tillie Regehr from Winnipeg, Manitoba, as well as several other relatives of Eichenfeld victims from B.C., Alberta, Manitoba, Ontario and the USA, have come to pay tribute to their slain relatives. Our bus draws up on a field and a local man says, "Oh yes, a cemetery was over there, up the hill where the lilac bushes are." A university research group from the city of Dnepropetrovsk has discovered remnants of this Mennonite cemetery in Petersdorf.

We string out on a cowpath through a pasture dotted with silvery Russian Olive bushes, pass a pond, several tethered red cattle and wade through high grass to reach the lilac grove, their flowers brown and spent. A recent excavation reveals an object. Could it be? Eager hands clear off dirt and we scan the slab. Yes, it is a tombstone, one with clear lettering reading "Johann Peters." Anita's great-grandfather. He died before the revolution, before the massacre. He got a stone. There must be other tombstones beneath the lilacs or perhaps they were removed to serve as foundation stones or road fill? Flushed, someone exclaims, "They could be dug out!"

In Petersdorf in October 1919, nine men, five of them Peters and two Regehrs were murdered. Three other Peters family men were killed in the nearby hamlet of Paulsheim.

Walking down we meet a woman wearing a man's brown fedora and a man in baggy pants. Curious, they have climbed the hill to see what these strangers, obviously North Americans, are doing in their pasture. Our Intourist guide explains the quest in Russian and the woman nods to the group and removes her hat.

Franzfeld is next to Petersdorf and here three of our group pose in front of their mother and aunt's Mennonite high school, a remarkably fine building, well preserved and still in use, a teachers' building next door. Acacia trees line the street, their pink and white clusters of bloom snowing petals. This peaceful village street once bustled with horses and buggies, carriages, farmers in harvest wagons, carts, children, girls in long dresses, boys in belted tunics and stiff caps. Now the cuckoo bird calls, dogs bark and roosters crow. A goat at the roadway strains at its rope.

The one-time Nickolaipole Mennonite highschool.

In Hochfeld, once so well-to-do, Charlotte Penner weeps as she finds her grandmother's house and the present owner, a cheery woman in a yellow kerchief, red, blue and green sweater and flowered skirt says, "Yes. You may go inside." Pure white pillows are on her bed, a rug on the wall, but hers is only half the house. She was an *Ostarbeiter*, she confides, taken away and forced as a young girl to work in Germany during WWII.

A Ukrainian village, once Dubovka now Novopetrovka, has replaced Eichenfeld. The memorial is not in the village, but at an intersection of two country roads, an open field be-

Charlotte Penner of Winnipeg (right) visits her parents' former home in Nickolaipole.

side the copse of bushes and trees that covers the mass graves at the end of the still existing cemetery. Some of our group walk through the village to the site, a memorial walk to remember the 82 persons murdered in this place.

A large crowd of people is already assembled around the marker. Aleksandr Pankeev, the master stonemason who carved the granite memorial, has come. Local villagers, some in worn cloth slippers and headscarves, others in high heels carrying bouquets of flowers, men in suits, people from the greater neighbourhood, all mix with people pouring out of chartered buses. Who knows them all? Close to the granite marker stand the relatives of Eichenfeld victims, the local dignitaries, intourist interpreter/guides and speakers. Buses from Zaporozhe have brought that city's Mennonite church members, their families and its church board chair Boris Letkeman. Steve Shirk,

Master Stonemason Aleksandr Pankeev (right) produced the memorial, which was designed by Paul Epp.

Mennonite Central Committee representative for Ukraine and Russia, is here to chair the memorial event. Herb and Maureen Klassen, first directors of the Mennonite Centre Ukraine, have come from Molochansk where they are overseeing the Mädchenschule renovation. Once the girls' high school in the Mennonite "capital" called Halbstadt, the school was purchased by Mennonites from abroad to offer aid and social services to local Ukrainians.

We see people from Zaporozhe and Dnepropetrovsk museums, from the region's universities, the central and regional archives, and village, municipal and regional officials. A bus from Dnepropetrovsk brings academics studying the Mennonite story. The media is represented by reporters and large cameras. An Orthodox priest in a long black cassock has been invited ("He looks so fresh, so young." "Only thirty," says Boris). Mennonite

Mennonite Minister Eduard Nachtigal and Ukrainian Orthodox Priest Vasili Kalyn reflect on the memorial ceremony.

historians and preachers, some three hundred people from Ukraine and abroad encircle the stone monument.

The dedication ceremony takes place outdoors, guests and participants standing for two hours on newly scythed grass. The memorial service is the first public mourning these victims of the Makhnovite terror have received. It is the first time their names and ages have been read out and they have had hymns sung, prayers and speeches said at this granite memorial in front of the dense thicket that covers their mass graves. Paul Epp of Toronto has designed the monument as a gray granite slab resting on two blocks of stone to suggest "the coffin on trestles these people never had and the dignified public viewing which they did not receive."

All parts of the memorial service have symbolic overtones. Speaking in the German used by the Mennonite victims and their families, and in Russian, the language used by most per-

Ukrainian villagers and Mennonite visitors attend the May 27, 2001 memorial ceremony.

sons in the area then and today, Steve Shirk of MCC opens the ceremony. The memorial stone is unveiled by Tina Breul from Winnipeg, a representative of the victims' families, and by a member of the local village community. There are reflections by historian Fedor Turchenko from Zaporozhe and a homily by John B. Toews, professor at Regent College, Vancouver. Prayers are offered by the Ukrainian Orthodox priest, a Mennonite minister working in Ukraine, and Herbert Klassen, co-director of the Mennonite Centre Ukraine. Hymns are sung in English, German, Ukrainian and Russian. The crowd is hushed as relatives or family members read out each name and age of the dead. One woman in the tour group counts 37 of the 136 names as her relatives. Members in the audience gasp to hear how young some victims were, how all males in some families were slain, how visiting male and especially female missionaries were slaughtered.

A memorial brochure, "In Sorrowful Remembrance," recalls that in 1919 the victims "could not be openly mourned or buried with dignity" and "affirms that violence has no place in human relations." It acknowledges that survivors, families of the massacred and the Mennonite community need to address their deep hurts, the trauma occasioned by the terror, the grief with which they have lived. It quotes eyewitnesses.

Fedor Turchenko, chair of History at the University of Zaporozhe and a noted specialist on the history of the region, recalls that Mennonites had lived together peacefully with Ukrainians "with whom they had found common understanding." John B. Toews, from Vancouver, speaks about finding a better way than violence: "We are all created in the image of God. In the name of Christ whom Mennonites, Orthodox and Baptists honour, we want to speak words of love and peace to one another." Head of Zaporozhe Intourist, Larissa Goryacheva, suggests that Mennonites coming back in such an open and dignified manner to memorialize their victims of the civil war will have a big impact on Ukraine. "Now I fully understand the Mennonite story."

Mikhail Sidorenko, head of the Zaporizhe Region Committee for Protection of Public Monuments, is overwhelmed that Mennonites have come in this way to publicly honour their innocent dead. It is "not in a spirit of anger or vengeance, but to honour the lives of their dead and to forgive the perpetrators." He notes that this is the first memorial to *victims,* not to heroes of the civil war. Ukrainians should also remember their innocent dead, he says. Harvey Dyck, historian, co-chair of the International Mennonite Memorial Committee for the Former

Soviet Union, long time researcher in Ukraine and organizer of this memorial project, states that Eichenfeld marks the beginning of several such projects to also honour innocent Mennonite victims of Soviet repression and terror. He notes that this event, in a spirit of understanding, for the first time brings together local and North American relatives and families of the Eichenfeld massacre victims with some area villagers whose ancestors may have participated in the looting that followed the killings. He reports that a central memorial for the some thirty percent of all Mennonites who perished in Soviet times is being planned.

After decades of being afraid to talk of the Soviet past, present members of the Zaporozhe Mennonite church and their Ukrainian friends welcome the public recognition of their past suffering and humiliation. They observe that Mennonites are returning to offer aid rather than to ask for recompense or retribution and that local Ukrainian academics and schools are now teaching the history of Mennonites in the settlement and development of the region. "Mennonites are gaining back their good name," they say, smiling. Jacques Kornberg from Toronto, a Holocaust specialist and friend of the Tsarist and Soviet Mennonite story, has suggested that Mennonites seem "less interested in pursuing perpetrators than in honouring the lives of those murdered."

At the end of the ceremony villagers bring their flowers—bright peonies, carnations, field flowers or plastic frilled nosegays—and reverently place them on the memorial slab till it resembles a raw grave piled high with funeral flowers.

At one corner of the clearing, in an echo of a funeral meal, women of the village have set tables and benches for a memo-

The Widows' Walk: Memorial participants retrace the path of the women and children who fled Eichenfeld on the night of the massacre.

rial reception that follows the dedication service. Pastries (*piroshky*) and drinks set on tables are offered to all guests.

In a final tribute to the Eichenfeld victims, retracing the flight and honouring the widows and orphans who stumbled together this way, fleeing the horrors of that terrible Sunday, people who attend the dedication slowly walk the two-kilometres from Eichenfeld to the village of Adelsheim.

The Eichenfeld memorial marks a significant new stage in acknowledging the long repressed history of the Mennonites of the Soviet Union. In 2001 Nestor Makhno is featured as a Ukrainian hero, an entire room being dedicated to him in the museum in Zaporozhe. The eyewitness accounts, grim, stark details of the murders in Eichenfeld, Ukrainian scholars see "as a bold step. We welcome it. It will lead to debate. We are recovering the truth of our history."

Chapter 2
Narrative and Analysis

Eichenfeld village was founded in 1869 on rich black soil overlooking the Dnieper River, 20 kilometres south of Khortitsa. It was part of the Iazykovo Daughter Settlement—the Old Colony planned its Daughters for success, choosing thirty-seven industrious, financially stable families as the first Eichenfelders.

In the following five decades the Eichenfelders worked hard and prospered. Dnieper River cargo boats and a steadily expanding network of railways carried their grain to Black Sea ports and onward to burgeoning international markets. Entrepreneurial Mennonites built wagons and windmills, stores and blacksmith shops to serve their growing community. A few Eichenfelders grew truly wealthy, purchased estates along the Dnieper, and built grand homes.

Eichenfeld was twenty years old in 1889 when, 100 kilometres to the southeast, in the Ukrainian village of Guliaipole, Nestor Ivanovich Makhno was born. Guliaipole was a successful town in its own right; its farms fed the same international markets as did Eichenfeld, and its shops and stores prospered in the same booming Ukrainian economy. But the Makhno family did not prosper.

Nestor's father, a peasant coachman employed by a wealthy merchant, died in 1890, leaving the eleven-month-old baby and his three brothers to be raised by their mother. It was a hard existence, and Nestor would soon be doing his part to help the family survive. By the age of seven he worked in the village herding cattle and sheep, and from the age of twelve he worked full time on local estates owned by wealthy Russians, Mennonites, and others.

Makhno was thirty and Eichenfeld was fifty when their histories intertwined so tragically on October 26, 1919. That Saturday, approximately 400 men riding under Makhno's black banner descended upon Eichenfeld. When they departed a day later, they left behind 75 murdered Mennonites. Over the following ten days, Makhno's men murdered seven more Eichenfelders. After the massacre the surviving Mennonite villagers buried their dead in twelve unmarked mass graves and fled the village. Neighbouring Ukrainian villagers came to loot abandoned belongings, and eventually took even the bricks of the empty Mennonite homes. Later, the Ukrainian village of Dubovka (now renamed Novopetrovka) expanded to encompass the site of vanished Eichenfeld.

Another eighty-two years passed before Mennonites returned to Eichenfeld to give the victims of the massacre a proper burial service. At the May 27, 2001 ceremony, descendants of Makhno's victims joined with Ukrainian villagers from Novopetrovka and the surrounding district and other concerned people from Ukraine and abroad to dedicate a memorial to those who died at Eichenfeld and in other civil war massacres in Nikolaipole district.

The memorial at Eichenfeld has at last properly laid the victims of the massacre to rest. But the history of the massacre and the events that led to it has yet to be told properly. Fragments of that history are gathered together in this memorial booklet, along with the names of the victims and the text of sermons and speeches from the memorial service. With the restoration of the memory of the victims' names, it is time also to begin the reconstruction of the events that engulfed them.

The Russian Revolution of 1905 saw violent peasant revolts sweep through the Russian empire. The peasants had no systematic political agenda. Their demands were simple and direct: land enough to support themselves; and liberty from taxation, conscription, and state interference in their day-to-day lives. This was naïve anarchism, unconcerned with the complexities of a modernizing world.

Peasants in Guliaipole were not immune to the passions of 1905, although the town avoided the most serious revolutionary violence. Nevertheless, in the aftermath of the revolution Tsarist retribution was indiscriminate, and residents of Guliaipole suffered equally with more rebellious peasants from other districts. A detachment of mounted police terrorized the town, brutally beating peasants and arresting anyone suspected of anti-tsarist sentiments.

Nestor Makhno turned sixteen in 1905, and the combination of revolutionary fervour and post-revolutionary tsarist brutality that he witnessed marked the beginning of his political activism.[1] He joined a small Anarchist-Communist group that distributed pamphlets, smuggled arms, assassinated tsarist officials, and robbed wealthy merchants and estate owners to finance their activities. In late 1906 tsarist police arrested Makhno for murder, but they could not find sufficient evidence and they soon released him. In 1908 the police again arrested Makhno, and this time, after he spent almost two years in jail awaiting trial, a military court sentenced him and thirteen fellow anarchists to death.

Makhno was not yet twenty when he was sentenced to death, and the court took mercy on him because of his age, commuting his sentence to life imprisonment in the infamous Butyrki prison in Moscow. There, over the following seven years, he received what passed for his formal education. The well-known anarchist Peter Arshinov, a fellow prisoner, introduced Makhno to anarchist literature, along with Russian grammar, literature, history, and geography. These years in Butyrki gave Makhno's anarchism a gloss of intellectual sophistication, but he would later admit that at heart his political beliefs retained their original naïve peasant character.

On 2 March 1917 the Russian Provisional Government celebrated Tsar Nicholas II's abdication with a general amnesty for political prisoners. Makhno, now twenty-seven, left Butyrki prison and returned to Guliaipole were he threw himself into revolutionary activities. His time in Butyrki lent him prestige among radicals in Guliaipole, and by the end of March he was chair of a newly created anarchist Peasant Union. Soon he also chaired the local Agricultural Committee, the Union of Metal and Carpentry Workers, and the Medical Union. Makhno's rise to regional power was underway.

Makhno's political aims were simple. He wanted to drive all landowners and political authorities out of the region, and transfer all land to the peasants to administer in their own interests as they saw fit. Although Makhno welcomed anarchist intellectuals into the ranks of his followers and gave them free reign to promote more sophisticated versions of anarchism, his own political aims never veered from this simple agenda.[2]

Makhno was a charismatic leader, and his call for local peasant rule found many sympathetic listeners. By late summer 1917 he was leading an armed band of peasants in raids on local landlords, including Mennonite and other German-speaking estate owners, and even rich peasants. His followers soon became known as the "Makhnovites," and they called their leader "Bat'ko"—"Little Father." From the outset, these raids were characterized by extreme violence; those who tried to resist faced brutal beatings and, sometimes, summary execution.

Makhno stood for opposition to all outside authority in the Guliaipole region. In the summer of 1917, this meant that his principal opponent was the Central Rada, the independent Ukrainian government that had formed in the wake of the February Revolution. When the Bolsheviks seized power in Russia in October 1917 and immediately promised to turn over all agricultural land to the peasants, the new regime appeared to be a natural ally to Makhno, but when the Bolsheviks launched their invasion of Ukraine in early 1918, the situation in southern Ukraine became far more complicated.

Now began the negotiations and machinations that were a central feature of Makhno's success in the coming three years. Southern Ukraine was a civil war battlefield with constantly shifting front lines. Soldiers from the White and Red Armies, Ukrainian nationalists (sometimes supported by Austrian and German allies), and the Makhnovites relied on the local inhabitants to provide food, clothing, horses, wagons and recruits. As the Bolsheviks fought successive Ukrainian nationalist regimes for control of Ukraine, Makhno played one side against the other. His ability to raise and lead peasant armies made him an invaluable ally and a dangerous enemy. Makhno sometimes fought on the side of Ukrainian nationalists, sometimes on the side of the Bolsheviks, never on the side of the White Army, and always for regional autonomy.

This multi-sided no-holds-barred conflict within a political vacuum, where peasants rampaged and no contending party exercised authority, provided the general setting of anarchy for the Eichenfeld massacre. But beyond the turmoil of civil war, the massacre occurred in the specific circumstance of General Anton Denikin's growing power in the late summer and autumn of 1919. Denikin, a prominent anti-Bolshevik figure, inherited leadership of the anti-Bolshevik Volunteer Army on the death of General Mikhail Alekseev in November 1918 and enjoyed sporadic success over the following nine months. When the Allied Powers began supplying Denikin with significant military aid in August 1919, his forces rapidly grew into a major threat to Bolshevik power. That autumn, Denikin seemed poised to push the Bolsheviks altogether out of southern Russia and Ukraine. By mid-October, his forces held a line running from Voronezh in the east, through Orel, Chernigov, and Kiev, to Odessa in the west. Denikin now publicly boasted that he would capture Moscow by the end of winter.[3]

Denikin stood unequivocally for the restoration of the old order in Russia, including the resumption of tight Russian control of Ukraine. For Makhno, this was intolerable, and he now focused his efforts on fighting the Volunteer Army. Makhno's position deep in the heart of Denikin-controlled territory would become strategically crucial in the ultimate defeat of the Volunteer Army.

Makhno found willing supporters in the villages of West Bank Ukraine, who feared Denikin's anti-Ukrainian policies. Makhno also gained the support of Ukrainians who had joined the Red Army to fight Denikin and now deserted the Bolsheviks as the Red Army retreated in disorder from Ukraine. By October 1919, Makhno's forces may have reached a total strength of 100,000 (although the exact numbers are the subject of much dispute).

In autumn 1919 Denikin's forces were badly over-extended, and Makhno took advantage of the situation to stage a major military action. On 5 October he captured Aleksandrovsk (Zaporizhe), and in the following two weeks took control of Ekaterinoslav and all the lower Dnieper, as well as the territory east of the river as far as the port city of Mariupol' on the Sea of Azov. Denikin was now forced to turn his attention to the rear and deal with Makhno.

Makhno's success brought new challenges for the partisan leader. For the first time he enjoyed fully independent control of a large territory, and this created unaccustomed civil administration responsibilities. Makhno, a skilled military commander, had little experience with civil administration, and to deal with his new responsibilities he convened the anarchist Fifth Congress of the Revolutionary Military Committee in Aleksandrovsk from 20-26 October 1919.[4]

The Congress, chaired by the well-known Anarchist Volin (AKA Boris M. Eichenbaum), organized committees of peasants, workers, and partisans to deal with civil administration, and then turned its attention to the immediate demands of defending Makhno's territory. Desperate shortages of military supplies prompted the Congress to organize local commissions of working people and partisans to provide food for the troops. These commissions were told to acquire supplies through "contributions" from the bourgeoisie and wealthy landowners within their territory. Makhno, of course, had begun his political career in 1905 forcibly raising such "contributions."

In the last months of 1919 Makhno's force occupied a huge swath of land, an area measuring 50 by 150 kilometres, along the east bank of the Dnieper River from Ekaterinoslav to Nikopol. The area embraced four multi-village Mennonite settlements with around 18,000 people. This included the Nikolaipole volost and its doomed village of Eichenfeld. Historian David G. Rempel lived through the Makhnovite occupation and writes:

> Throughout the bandit-held corridor all Mennonites faced the same terror. Like wild beasts the Makhnovites stormed into all but the poorest houses, ransacking and stealing anything in sight–clothing, bedding, pillows, curtains, dishes, food, and of course horses and wagons. No matter what time of the day or night, the plundering always began with the command, 'Mistress (*khoziaika*), prepare us a meal and be quick about it.' [5]

By October 1919, Eichenfeld, now in Makhno's territory, had suffered along with the rest of southern Ukraine through two long years of civil war hardships. Prosperous Mennonite villages naturally attracted the attention of all combatants, who looked to local communities for supplies. Makhno's success in the autumn of 1919, the resultant civil administration demands, the immediate danger of Denikin's military response, and the Fifth Congress's decision to supply the Makhnovites through "contributions" from wealthy landowners, were together an ominous confluence of circumstances for the Eichenfelders.

The final, fatal element in this confluence was probably the presence in Eichenfeld of Heinrich Heinrichs. In spite of pacifist religious convictions, some desperate Mennonites had followed the example of their Ukrainian neighbours and formed armed self-defense units (*Selbschutzabteilungen*) to protect their communities. Heinrichs, a leader in the Mennonite self-defense movement, made his home in Eichenfeld. He would be the Makhnovites's first Eichenfeld victim.

On Saturday, October 26, 1919, a band of roughly 400 Makhno troops arrived in Eichenfeld. Makhno was not with them, and it cannot be proved that he directly ordered their activities that day. Still, their disciplined, purposeful actions and clear-cut criteria in singling out their victims bespoke careful planning, and in Makhno's territory, Makhno was the chief planner. Makhno exercised close military discipline over his forces, and it is almost unimaginable that the Makhnovites carried out the massacre without his approval.[6]

Two elements of the Eichenfeld massacre reveal careful planning. To begin with, when the Makhnovites arrived that Saturday morning, their first action was to find and kill Heinrichs. In the midst of Makhno's struggle with Denikin, and in the context of Makhno's attempt to assert firm control over the region, this execution of a prominent leader in the self-defense movement was surely an intentionally symbolic act. The Eichenfeld massacre was a warning to Mennonites throughout the region that Makhno would not tolerate resistance.

A second clear indication of planning was the careful selection of victims. Many accounts of the massacre agree that the Makhnovites singled out landowners as their main victims. The principal exception to this, the slaughter of six members of a tent mission, remains unexplained. Makhno had targeted wealthy landowners since 1905, and the Fifth Congress had identified landowners as the main source for contributions to the Makhnovites. On the night of October 26-27, as the Makhnovites moved from house to house murdering landowners, the message that landowners everywhere would perish was unequivocal.

The brutality of the massacre, the terror that the survivors experienced, the flight to neighbouring villages, and the return to hurriedly bury the bodies, are related in stark detail in the first-hand accounts reproduced in this booklet. Nothing more can be accomplished by repeating them here.

It remains to briefly describe the fate of Makhno and his men. Makhno's autumn 1919 campaign played a strategically pivotal role in the defeat of General Denikin. Already over-extended, Denikin's Volunteer Army was poorly prepared to deal with a major insurrection at its rear. While Denikin chased Makhno, the Red Army regrouped and, under the leadership of Leon Trotsky, began its long, slow push to final victory. Denikin withdrew southward, and Makhno proved unable to stand against the main forces of the retreating Volunteer Army. The Makhnovites abandoned Ekaterinoslav to Denikin on December 8 and retreated to the region of Aleksandrovsk and Melitopol.

In late December Red Army troops entered Aleksandrovsk, and Makhno once again allied himself with the Bolsheviks. However, with Denikin withdrawn to the Crimea, and his Volunteer Army melting away, it would not take long for Makhno and the Bolsheviks to recognize that their aims were incompatible. In January 1920 the Bolsheviks outlawed Makhno, and in March they organized a special force to fight the Makhnovites.

Over the following year, a desperate Makhno briefly flirted with an alliance with the Volunteer Army, now led by General Peter Wrangel, before once again allying with the Bolsheviks against Wrangel in October 1920. This was a short-lived alliance. With the defeat of Wrangel in November, the Bolsheviks no longer needed Makhno, and turned against him once and for all. Makhno's supporters were now reduced to a small handful of loyalists, who held out through the winter months and on into the summer of 1921. Makhno and eighty-three followers finally slipped across the Dniester River into Romania on 28 August 1921. After periods of internment in Romania and Poland, Makhno made his way to Paris, where he died of tuberculosis in 1934.

When Makhno fled Ukraine, he left behind a confused legacy. To some Ukrainian peasants he was a legendary figure, a kind of modern-day Robin Hood. To Soviet historians he was a bandit, an image that persists strongly among Ukrainian peasants in the villages surrounding one-time Eichenfeld. In the post-Soviet era, some Ukrainian nationalists have adopted him as a national hero because of his resistance to the Bolsheviks.

To Mennonites, he is a nightmarish figure who brought wanton suffering and death to the innocent.[7] During the Civil War around a percent and a half of Mennonites empire-wide died from violence, close to the national average. But in areas occupied by Makhnovites the direct losses exceeded five percent. Yet as a mainly religious community Mennonites viewed Makhnovite butchery equally as the scourge of God, as recompense for their moral failings. But whether interpreted as deserved or not, suffering triggered a powerful revivalist, penitential mood among Mennonites that shaped their outlook for decades to come.

The Mennonite perspective is understandable. The Eichenfeld massacre was not an isolated incident, but was part of a larger pattern of attacks on Mennonites. To a degree this reflects the general prosperity of Mennonite communities, which made them an obvious target for confiscations. The heartland from which Makhno drew ninety percent of his following was enveloped by large and wealthy settlements, mainly Mennonite, but including Lutheran and Catholic German villages and estates. Here was a rich and strategically situated supply base of horses, wagons, fodder, food, clothes and money for the Makhnovtsi.[8] After Makhno's occupation of Aleksandrovsk in late 1919, district officials reported that the Makhnovites had confiscated 2643 horses, 2082 head of cattle, 1213 pigs, and almost five million kilograms of grain.[9] Officials concluded that the "horrific spree of the occupying Makhno army . . . based primarily in the villages of the [Mennonite] Khortitsa volost for three months, reduced the once-wealthy region to the verge of poverty."[10]

The Mennonites' prosperity identified them as targets, but this does not alone explain the ferocity of the attacks, which embraced whoever and whatever was at hand in the area of Makhnovite occupation. During the occupation of Aleksandrovsk, the Makhnovites murdered sixty-five people, raped ninety-two women, "beat and brutalized" 379 people, and burned forty-four houses.[11] Elsewhere the toll was equally brutal. At the village of Ebenfeld, Borosenko Mennonite settlement, the Makhnovites slaughtered 67 Mennonite men, women, and children.[12] Other bloody attacks came in the Zagradovka and Schönfeld Mennonite settlements. As members of a German-speaking ethno-religious and ethno-cultural minority, Mennonites were persecuted as German-speaking outsiders after having been stereotyped and scapegoated by wartime propaganda as enemies of Mother Russia.

They were not the only ones, for other minorities also suffered at the hands of Makhno and his followers. Jews, in particular, were targets. As a Bolshevik official reported following a November 1920 trip to meet with Makhno in Guliaipole, the rank-and-file Makhnovites talked of almost nothing but the "battle with Bolsheviks and Jews."[13] In one instance, in a December 1919 Makhnovite raid on the city of Berdiansk, almost 100 Jews were singled out and murdered.[14] The Makhnovites also targeted landlords of all nationalities, village officials (most notably local Bolshevik and one-time Tsarist officials), and even wealthier peasants. During the Aleksandrovsk occupation, the Makhnovites "altogether leveled" the well-off Ukrainian peasant villages of Ternovatoe and Vladimirovka.[15]

In light of all of these depredations, the popular image of Makhno deserves a close reexamination. As already noted, this image is partially a product of post-Soviet Ukraine's search for national heroes. Makhno's anti-Bolshevik escapades have been adopted by some Ukrainians as an element of popular Ukrainian nationalist mythology.[16] But Makhno's legend extends into mainstream Western historiography too, where he appears as a romantic man of the people, a Robin Hood figure, the "Pancho Villa of the Russian Revolution" in the words of one influential author.[17] The preponderance of such portrayals, set against the backdrop of the atrocities perpetrated by Makhno and his followers, makes a re-assessment of Makhno all the more pressing.

The massacre at Eichenfeld is an important part of the Makhno story as an extraordinarily well-documented and symptomatic event. Eighty-two murders may be a tiny drop in the ocean of death that engulfed southern Ukraine during the Civil War, but the circumstances that surrounded the

Eichenfeld massacre offer important insights into Makhno and his movement.

Makhno's success in October 1919 was transitory, made possible only by the over-extension of the Volunteer Army. He never commanded forces adequate to defeat a large and organized enemy, and his destructive administrative practices, based on arbitrary confiscations and on making bloody examples of anyone who opposed him, offered no basis for establishing a permanent civil administration. Depredations, at Eichenfeld and elsewhere, were not signs of Makhno's power, but of his desperation.

The history of Makhno and of Eichenfeld intersected tragically on October 26-27, 1919. The Makhnovites destroyed Eichenfeld over the course of those two days. Within two years, the Makhnovites themselves were destroyed, victims of Soviet power. Finally, with the destruction of the Soviet Union, Mennonites and Ukrainians have returned to the site of the massacre to honour and grieve the dead. This book is a record of that massacre and of the May 27, 2001 service in its memory. It is also, we hope, a first step toward a deeper understanding of the Eichenfeld tragedy and of the larger revolutionary world that gave it shape.

Notes

[1] The general biography of Makhno, sketched here, is well documented. English-language biographical accounts of Makhno include Michael Palij, *The Anarchism of Nestor Makhno, 1918-1921: An Aspect of the Ukrainian Revolution* (Seattle: University of Washington Press, 1976), 67-74; and Victor Peters, *Nestor Makhno: The Life of an Anarchist* (Winnipeg: Echo Books, 1970). A more detailed account can be found in Alexandre Skirda, *Nestor Makhno, le cosaque libertaire (1888-1934): La*

guerre civile en Ukraine 1917-1921 (Paris: Les Editions de Paris, 1999), 27-48. A prominent Ukrainian account is Valerii Volkovins'kii, *Nestor Makhno: legendi I real'nist'* (Kiev: Perlit Prodakshn, 1994), 5-26.

[2] On Makhno's ideology, see Skirda, *Nestor Makhno*, 393; A. V. Timoshchuk, *Anarkho-kommunisticheskie formirovaniia N. Makhno (septiabr' 1917-avgust 1921 g.)* (Simferopol: Tavria, 1996); Palij, *The Anarchism of Nestor Makhno*, 3.

[3] The best account of the military situation in southern Ukraine is Aleksandr Shubin, *Makhno I makhnovskoe dvizhenie* (Moscow: MIK, 1998). Palij, *The Anarchism of Nestor Makhno*, provides a useful English-language overview.

[4] The best published account of the Congress is A.V. Shubin, *Anarkhitskiy sotsial'nyi eksperiment: Ukraina i Ispaniia 1917-1939 gg* (Moscow: RAN, 1998), 57-61. Anarchist Petr Arshinov, who played a leading role in the conference, describes it in very partisan terms in *Istoriia makhnovskogo dvizheniia (1918-1921)* (Zaporozhe: Dikoe Pole, 1995), 140-144. See also Palij, *The Anarchism of Nestor Makhno*, 196-197; Timoshchuk, *Anarkho-kommunisticheskie formirovaniia*, 84-88; Skirda, *Nestor Makhno,* 197-202.

[5] David G. Rempel with Cornelia Rempel Carlson, *A Mennonite Family in Tsarist Russia and the Soviet Union, 1789-1923* (University of Toronto Press, 2002), 222-3.

[6] On discipline in Makhno's forces, see Timoshchuk, *Anarkho-kommunisticheskie formirovaniia*, 89.

[7] Skirda, *Nestor Makhno*, 7-10, provides an excellent summary of the many different perceptions of Makhno. A more thorough historiographical account appears in V. D. Ermakov, *Rossiiskii anarchism i anarkhisty (vtoraia polvina XIX-konets XX vekov)* (St. Petersburg: Nestor, 1996), 39-50.

[8] Rempel, *Mennonite Family,* 184-5.

[9] "Dokladnaia zapiska Khortitskago Volrevkoma na Gubernskii s'ezd volostnykh i sel'skikh revkomov, i komnezamozhnei Aleksandrovskoi gubernii," 12 June 1920, *Zaporizhzhe Regional State Archive,* fond R73, opis 1, delo 47, pp. 63-67. The occupation is vividly portrayed in David G. Rempel with Cornelia Rempel Carlson, *A Mennonite Family in Tsarist Russia* (Toronto: University of Toronto Press, 2003), 208-251.

[10] "Dokladnaia zapiska Khortitskago Volrevkoma," 63-67.

[11] Ibid.

[12] For this data we are indebted to Dr. Peter Letkemann, Winnipeg.

[13] "Upolnomochennyi po poezdke v shtab Povstancheskikh voisk imeni Bat'ki Makhno N. Goppe," 18 November 1920, *Zaporizhzhe Regional State Archive,* fond R73, opis 1, delo 48, p 10-10ob.

[14] "Upolnomochennomu Vseukrainskago Komiteta pomoshchi Naseleniiu, Postradivshemu Ot Pogromov Po Aleksandrovskoi i Donetskoi Guberniam," 22 December 1920, *Zaporizhzhe Regional State Archive,* fond R73, opis 1, delo 69, p 9.

[15] "Dokladnaia zapiska Khortitskago Volrevkoma," pp. 63-67.

[16] Volkovins'kii, *Nestor Makhno,* is the most prominent example.

[17] Orlando Figes, *A People's Tragedy: The Russian Revolution 1891-1924* (London: PIMLICO, 1997), 662.

Chapter 3
The Memorial as Metaphor
Paul Epp

The concept for this memorial had its origin in the belief that a vertical, heroic element would be profoundly inappropriate for this memorial. The Eichenfeld tragedy needs to be remembered and the memory of its victims honoured. But this remembrance should not be clothed in anything hinting at celebration, however solemn. Gravestones celebrate completed lives. The lives of these victims were violently foreshortened and tragically incomplete.

I have been deeply touched by photographs of Mennonite victims of civil war violence reposing in their coffins, often slightly tilted, perhaps to benefit the camera. My design for the Eichenfeld memorial seeks to capture this sense of grief, dignity and remembrance. The grey granite slab resting on two granite trestles represents the coffin these Mennonite men, women, and children never had and the dignified public viewing they never received.

The position of the granite slab situated low to the ground requires that the observer bow his head in viewing it. This seems to me the most appropriate posture. Moreover, since this memorial is not easily noticeable from afar the viewer will need to search for it and experience the thrill of discovery on finding it. Symbolically this experience mimics the way we search in the past and seek meaning in it.

Part II
MENNONITE WITNESSES

Chapter 4
A Time of Darkness
Isaak Epp

In 1869 a group of Mennonites settled on land purchased for the landless by the Khortitsa district. It was located some thirty miles south of Ekaterinoslav on the west bank of the Dnieper River. Eventually five villages were founded there: Nikolaifeld/Nikolaipole, Franzfeld/Varvarovka, Hochfeld/Morozovka, Adelsheim/Dolinovka and Eichenfeld/Dubovka. The settlement was known as Iazikovo and constituted an independent Mennonite community. I was a teacher in the village of Eichenfeld/Dubovka for six years and I know the settlement well.

What follows is a report of the settlement's time of troubles. I will follow the notes of the current elder, Heinrich Epp, who lived through this period. It was a time of darkness. In a letter written prior to this period my father commented: "People are sewing wind and will reap the whirlwind." It was a time when everyone knew best, where no one wanted to be led by another.

At that time the word "Makhno" evoked terror. He was a freed prisoner with anarchist leanings. His home—Guliaipole—was a large village in Ukraine where all like-minded individuals gathered who were dissatisfied with existing conditions. Thanks to years of military service many people had forgotten how to work. The war itself made them insensitive and even brutal. For them there was nothing terrible about blood and death. Robbery and murder were taken for granted. "What I need or what I desire I must have"—that is the way these people thought. Everything belonged to them whether the clothes, bread or houses of the peaceable inhabitants or even their daughters or wives.

In the summer of 1919 thousands of these people marched westward in seemingly endless columns, but without causing too much damage. When they returned in September the robberies began. Many a person fell victim to their sabers and many a Mennonite village went up in flames. In the villages of Steinbach and Ebenfeld (near Nikolaithal, Borozenko Settlement), they did not even spare the babies in the cradle. I know one village in which virtually every girl fell victim to the ruthless hands of these devils in human form.

They arrived in Nikolaipole on October 12, 1919. On October 25 and 26 the Makhnovites marched through Ekaterinoslav in large numbers. Around noon on Saturday, October 26, a large number of their cavalry entered the village. In Nikolaipole Johann Klaassen was horribly beaten and slashed with sabers. He died a few hours later. In the waiting room of the doctor these same people shot the apothecary and a Heinrich Peters from Reinfeld who was waiting to see the doctor. (Reinfeld was a village near Nikolaipole in which several Mennonite estate owners lived. The village has been destroyed.) At the home of a postal employee they shot a Jewish student who had just arrived, and wounded a Pole from Galicia. Near the end of the village of Varvarovka they encountered Brother Reimer of the *Zeltmisson* (Tent Mission) who was entering the chemist's shop to get some drugs. They chased him into the machine shed of the bookseller Redekop and shot him. One bandit walked into the house and was met by Redekop. His wife escaped. "Are you a German?" he asked bluntly. "Yes I am." "We have orders to kill all Germans. " A shot was fired and Redekop fell dead. Then they murdered Peter Friesen, Jakob Quiring and his son Abraham. At other homes they threatened and abused people but no one else was murdered in Varvarovka. From here the terrorists went to Morozovka (Hochfeld) where they ravaged the village. They entered the yard of Kornelius Epp. Young Jakob Epp saw them coming and ran to the adjoining house where he and his young wife lived. "They are Makhnovites. I have to be with father," Jakob exclaimed.

They observed them readying their weapons. There was a shot. They had placed Jakob behind his father and killed both with a single bullet. Within two hours these fiends killed fifteen people. Among them was the aged and faithful minister Kornelius Lehn.

On Friday five persons from the Russian *Zeltmission* arrived in Eichenfeld. The missionary Dyck preached a moving sermon. During the afternoon cavalry riders entered the village. On Saturday morning militia arrived via the road from Petersdorf (Petersdorf was a settlement of Mennonite estate owners, located three miles south of Eichenfeld.) The column was endless. All day long they passed through the village, robbing at will. The Makhnovites were well organized and well armed: guns, sabers, daggers, revolvers, pistols, hand grenades, machine guns, cannons. In a well organized state one can hardly imagine this. But Russia, which even before the revolution was called a land of unlimited opportunities, provided every opportunity to organize a bandit army consisting of many thousands—this thanks to its disbanded and disorganized army. One should not suppose that only the lowest classes joined the movement. There were also educated people among them. Some suffered inwardly when they observed what their colleagues were doing but they could not leave.

Let's continue the story. An eyewitness reported:

My brother had to transport [some bandits] and only returned in the evening. Father had to prepare for the night guests. The barn and the storage shed were full of horses and the house full of men. Father looked after them as best he could. In the evening we received the news that Kornelius Pauls (my brother-in-law) had been shot. Then they brought Peter Pauls and shot him near the window of our summer room. Meanwhile my brother locked the student house. It was the last time we saw him alive. Father was in the attic where my frightened sister joined him. He stood in anguished prayer. Both came down and father sat down in the corner of the small room. There was silence. Suddenly he said: "This is terrible, I could never have imagined this." Then they came to get my dear dear father. He took my little sister in his arms and kissed her and my mother. The soldiers screamed at him and he could not say goodbye to the others.

He showed no fear, no trembling, no lack of courage. He walked out calmly and assuredly without once looking back. He never returned. "Don't run away. Stay with mother. Nothing will happen. I have prayed for you!" he told us daughters. On our knees we begged these men to return our father. They said he would be back tomorrow. During the night we encountered many dangers. The evil men were drunk and wanted women. That was horrible! How we prayed to God! And behold the prayer of our parents was answered. It was raining outside and the dogs were barking. A passing herd of cattle lowed. An ominous night after a terrible evening. Then what a horrible morning. Mother and her grown daughters, hollow eyed and white as snow, searched for their loved ones. No one could cry. We had lost too much: father, brother, friend—the entire village had been murdered.

Oh sorrow, oh what great sorrow.

Everything pointed to the fact that the massacre in Eichenfeld/Dubovka had been carefully organized. At one end of the village all home owners and their eldest sons (who could be captured) were hacked to death with sabers, at the other end all were shot. The two teachers H. Wiens and W. Peters were also murdered as were [*Zeltmission* members] J. Dyck (Halbstadt), O. Jushkevich (Riga), J. Golyzin (Mohilev), and the women R. Rosenberg, Konotop, and L. Hiebert (Rueckenau). In all seventy-five persons lost their lives during this night.

The news of this massacre spread rapidly. On October 28 two young men from Nikolaifeld/Nikolaipole (located four miles west of Eichenfeld/Dubovka) took courage and went to Eichenfeld. Thick fog covered the village and fields. It seemed as if the place itself wanted to hide the cruel deeds that had been perpetrated. Encouraging one another they neared this place of terror. As they approached they wondered: "What if you should die today!" They arrived at the end of the village. An uncanny feeling enveloped them as they walked down the street. Everything was deserted and empty. There was no life on any farm. Truly the silence of death! Here and there a dog ran furtively down the street. At one house the watchdog sat howling, bemoaning his loss. They walked to the school in the middle of the village without meeting a single person. Here they encountered the many widows and the few surviving men. They walked to the churchyard.

Most of the bodies lay covered in blood, only a few had been washed. Some of the bodies were so badly mutilated that they were unrecognizable. Most lay naked or only in a shift. The murder victims had been robbed of their clothing. Large graves had already been prepared. In these the bodies were laid close together—the son by the father, the relative by the relative. Most were laid in the grave as they were with only a little straw under their head. Very few were wrapped in sheets. Why? There was nothing left. Everything had been taken. The funeral was heart breaking. No tears were shed. The widows and orphans walked about the cemetery like shadows. The terror and the horrible deeds so overwhelmed human feelings that they were incapable of expressing themselves. You God above, you look into the sorrow and suffering of the broken human heart. You alone can and will comfort. Grant that on that great day of resurrection we may all arise and spend eternity with you. Amen.

After the dead were buried most families left Eichenfeld immediately, but unfortunately a few remained behind. On

November 2 (O.S.) bandits entered the village and murdered Jakob Friesen and David Friesen. On November 4 a young bandit killed the ill and old W. Pauls, hacked his mentally retarded son to death and shot Abraham Guenther. The youth Peter Block was murdered on November 6. On October 26 H. K. Peters, the teacher, P. Janzen, and an unknown person were murdered in Petersdorf. On November 5 three bandits killed the following, in Petersdorf: Fr. Peters and his son Johann and two refugees from Kronsweide, Mr. Regier and his son.

Wagons and several riders entered the yard of B. Dyck Jr. in Nikolaipole. Dyck went out to meet them.

"This face looks familiar. What's your name?"

"Dyck."

"No he is not the one. Who is your neighbour?"

He was named. "That's him."

The spokesperson ordered that the wagon drivers be shown hospitality. Then they left. At the D. F. Peters residence they carried on in the most brutal fashion. Between 8 PM and 2 AM they tortured, beat and slashed Peters. Completely drunk they forced him to swear, abused him and demanded money. He went with them to a speculator in order to borrow money. When these people did not immediately open the door they fired a shot through the door which killed young W. Schwarz. Later these same scoundrels wounded the youth Fr. Unruh so severely that he died at five o clock. Peters died at 2 AM. The murdering finally stopped but the robbing and plundering continued for a long time.

Various illnesses soon spread among the bandits. Worst of all was typhus. The illness was spread by lice. The bandits were dirty and full of vermin. Since they slept in all the beds there were enough lice to spread typhus. No one was safe. One after another became ill. Many died. The Nikolaipole community buried every fifth person.

Spring came to the land but who was there to plant and what was there to plant?

Notes

From Isaak Epp, "Dubowka," *Vorworts,* Vol. 21, no.51 (Dec. 21, 1923). Translated by John B. Toews.

Chapter 5
Eichenfeld under the Black Cloud
David A. Quiring

We knew that the Makhno forces had been active in the Old Colony (Khortitsa) for some weeks—terrorizing, burning and killing. Some were shot, some strangled, some hanged. Innocent Mennonites in Khortitsa lost their lives. We in the Nikolaipole district heard these horror stories day after day. Men and women, young and old, small and large—all were indescribably abused.

We prayed to God that He spare us, keep the bandits away from us and protect us from such murderous hands. We prayed that He would free Khortitsa from the power of darkness. We learned that these Makhnovites were moving through all the surrounding villages and estates. They also passed through Einlage where they robbed and destroyed.

They continued their evil work at *Bethania*, an institution for those with epilepsy. Even here the power of darkness did not spare the patients. They were terrorized, threatened and abused. Bedding, clothing and products were stolen, loaded on wagons and taken away.

They [the Makhnovites] then moved towards the center of the district to Neu-Kronsweide, a rather lovely village, wealthy by virtue of its farms. Once there they literally began to destroy the village. People were beaten, shot and stabbed. Then they began robbing. Those who survived fled on wagons, horses or on foot in an attempt to save their lives, leaving behind farms and all else. My brother-in-law moved from Neu-Kronsweide earlier. Our eighty-seven year old father stayed behind and was murdered in the most gruesome fashion by these fiends. He was beaten to death with a club. His nose was completely smashed, the clothes torn from his body and the body covered with bed feathers. I simply can't describe or picture this.

One night the survivors came to recover the bodies. There were nine corpses in Neu-Kronsweide. My brother-in-law drove to collect the body of our dear father. It was pitch dark when they entered the village and drove into the back yard. Quickly they ran into the house, collected the corpse and laid it on the wagon. A small boy drove the wagon while my brother-in-law and nephew walked some distance away. It was very muddy. As the boy was about to leave the village he was confronted by two bandits who stopped the wagon and asked who he had with him. He explained it was the body of his grandpa. The bandits wanted to throw the body off the wagon but finally yielded to the boy's pleas. They climbed aboard and drove with us as far as Einlage. Our uncle said it was impossible to bury the body in Einlage because of the bandits and so we continued our journey by night to Neuendorf where we buried father in the cemetery.

Once they had hauled virtually everything from the village of Neu-Kronsweide, they set it on fire. The Makhnovites now moved to the centre of the district. The bandits followed the road from Ekaterinsolav, to Alexandrovsk, a distance of 75 versts. I call these bandits the "black ones" for they carried a large black banner with "Death" inscribed in white letters.

The bandits reached the large, rich and beautiful estates in Petersdorf. I can't report everything these people did in terms of atrocities and murders, only that in the end they tortured and shot six men. They cut and hacked off the fingers of a certain Franz D. Peters, severely tortured him and then shot him. Then they robbed the estates.

You have no idea how we who were living nearby felt. We were frightened by all the terrible reports, especially as this dark cloud steadily approached. On October 25 the so-called *Zeltmission* [tent mission] was active in our vicinity. Five persons came to Eichenfeld to tell us of Jesus' great love and of salvation in Christ. Many responded. The leader of the *Zeltmission* was brother J. Dyck, who came with four other persons. Minister Schellenberg from Reinfeld accompanied them. They arrived at noon and at 3 PM they were invited to speak. Many from our village attended the service in the large school building. I too had the opportunity to attend. When I arrived the school was filled to capacity. I was happy that the Lord had succeeded in bringing so many thirsty souls together. As we learned later, for many it was the last chance.

Brother Dyck opened the service. Many beautiful, moving songs were sung in German and Russian. As we sat in the assembly listening to God's Word we heard the frightening news that several men of "the black cloud" were robbing the teacher's room, but they soon left and drove through the village and robbed a few farms. The service ended and an invitation was given to return at 6 PM.

After the service I walked over to my brother with whom I owned a rather large business. He informed me that the same

Makhnovites who had robbed the teacher's room also visited him. Uttering terrible threats they demanded he open the store. When he did so they all walked in and began to assault him. They threatened to shoot him unless he gave them thousands of rubles. Then they threw him in the cellar and continued to beat him. Finally he went to the cash register and gave them money. They fled to the street and climbed on the wagon. How pale and frightened my brother looked. The entire village was agitated. Everyone wondered what the night would bring.

Fear, alarm and uneasiness filled the inhabitants of the village as they walked down the street. I returned to my brother Johann. My family was also there as well as my mother-in-law and brother-in-law who had fled from Kronsweide the previous week. Several decided to go to the service, others stayed home in case the bandits paid a return visit. I went to the school which was filled to capacity. The service was again opened in German and Russian. It was beautiful. "Today if you hear His voice, harden not your hearts." It was a special hour. Towards the end of the service brother Dyck repeatedly invited people to come to Jesus. Many stood up to signify their desire to follow Jesus.

The service closed with an invitation to attend Bible Study at 9 AM at the residence of sister Mrs. Johann Peters. I went home to my family, mother-in-law and brother-in-law. An uncanny silence prevailed and we village inhabitants dreaded the coming night. We were fearful but our prayers and pleading during family devotions brought us comfort and strength. We gave ourselves over to God's protection and care for the coming night. With God's help the night passed peaceably, but in the morning we were uneasy.

After breakfast I went to the street and saw a Makhnovite on horseback. He was a scout keeping watch for his regiment following several miles behind. I quickly disappeared when I saw a mounted Makhnovite wearing a large, brown coat and armed to the teeth. I informed my family and soon we witnessed the regiments organized in hundreds entering our village. They did not stop at my [brother's] residence since it was not a farm. The streets were soon filled. Finally a buggy drawn by three horses and carrying four armed Makhnovites entered our driveway. Two of them jumped off the wagon and burst into the room. Swearing and yelling they demanded *borshch* and *Rollkuchen* and ordered we feed the horses two pails of oats. No sooner said than done.

My wife had prepared the *borshch* earlier. Quickly she prepared the *Rollkuchen*. The bandits sat down and ate without complaint. Then they noticed the guitar in the room and asked who could play. I informed them it was my wife and they requested she play. I told her to play. She played and sang the first verse. We began to sing the second verse when one of them asked us to stop for two of them had tears in their eyes. They asked if we couldn't play something more lively. We replied that we could not. The men had very piercing eyes and we dared not look at them directly. We feared they might become more demanding but they did not. They got up, hitched their horses and drove away.

Thousands of men marched through the village between 9 AM and 4 PM. Thousands of sheep and cattle accompanied them. Right after lunch several bandits entered the yard of our neighbour Heinrich Heinrichs. He came out to meet them in a friendly fashion but they only screamed at him.

I walked into the village where our store was located in order to see what was going on. I soon discovered that several Makhnovites had found my brother Johann and were beating and assaulting him. I did not dare go in and made a hasty retreat. All the yards were filled with Makhnovites. I got safely home only to discover that Heinrichs had been shot. My brother-in-law Heinrich now decided to take our mother-in-law to their house in Nikolaipole for Sunday. As things turned out he was fortunate.

Towards evening the column thinned somewhat. Seven men wanted to spend the night and of course we had to agree. Three more bandits appeared and demanded that my [other] brother-in-law Peter, whose horses were standing in the yard, offer them transport. He was hesitant but they threatened him with their weapons. He hitched the horses [to the wagon] and they drove off.

It grew dark. I went inside and looked through the window to the street. A large regiment of Makhnovite cavalry approached at full gallop. They stopped briefly near the yard next to the blacksmith shop but then rode into the village.

Fearfully we awaited what the darkness would bring. Suddenly my cousin appeared. It was D. Woelk, the head of the village council. He asked me to trade places with him. He was exhausted since he had to run errands for the bandits throughout the day and requested I walk through the village ordering people to bake bread for the military throughout the night. I was about to leave when brothers Jakob and Klaas came from the village and informed us they had to collect straw for the cattle of the Makhnovites. Brother Jakob told us that many people in the village had been shot. I felt numb but since I promised my cousin, I left to broadcast the order.

I walked from yard to yard even though I felt fear and trepidation. The village teemed with Makhnovites. When I entered one yard I was surrounded by Makhnovites. They readied their weapons to fire on me. But the hand of the Most High prevented this. When I informed them of my mission they let me pass.

I continued on my way and came to the yard of Sister Mrs. Johann Peters. The yard was filled with horses tied to the fences. The riders were in the house with Sister Peters. I only dared to go as far as the barn door, then left to fulfill my further obligations. In the middle of the village, I arrived at my brother Johann's, where there were many Makhnovites. I was certain they would stop me so I walked up to them and asked permission to enter the yard and announce the order to bake bread. They granted permission. When I stepped into the front room the bandits surrounded me, screaming and swearing. I told them of my mission and they allowed me to enter the bedroom where I saw my sister-in-law Ina and her mother. They informed me that my brothers Peter and Johann had been shot. I pretended not to hear them, announced the order in Russian and left. I cannot describe how I felt.

Momentarily I was uncertain what to do, but then I continued walking into danger. At one yard they asked me how I dared to walk on the street. "I have to," I responded. Now and then I heard gunfire. Many inhabitants were being shot as I walked through the village. I hardly knew what to do in my anxiety but I still stopped at several yards. As I approached the Franz Klassen home a number of bandits were standing on the street. I could not walk around them so I walked directly towards them. I excused myself and asked for permission to enter the yard. "Go ahead," they retorted, swearing and making fun of me. Two men followed me as I walked on to the yard. I heard the clicks as they readied their guns. As I entered the doorway I stopped. The hallway was full of these murderers. As I later learned, the owner, Franz Klassen, had already been shot. Near the barn door two men from our village were about to be executed. One was Julius Lehn. I stood among these ruthless robbers for a few minutes. Then they ordered the two to walk from the barn door to the straw stack—the place of execution.

Suddenly they shouted: "Get rid of this man." They struck me on the head so that the blood ran. How I prayed to God from the depth of my being to save me from these murderous hands. I can still feel the fear in my heart. Wondrously the Holy and Almighty hand did not allow them to kill me. I was almost at the straw stack with my murderer when he took me by the arm and said I had to see the commander. He led me through the hallway into the room where I stood and waited. The commander was in the bedroom where he was abusing Mrs. Klassen and her old mother. After a few minutes he stormed into the room screaming and swearing. I prayed fervently to our gracious Lord for strength and grace to endure what lay ahead. The commander placed his revolver against my temple. His other gun, a Browning, was tucked in his belt. "Who are you? Do you have any land?" Everyone was asked that question. I answered that I had neither land nor a house, a statement verified by Mrs. Franz Klassen. I was freed and he ordered his soldier to escort me to the street. It was completely dark when he brought me to the other side of the street. Now I did not know what to do and stood there in fear. Should I fulfill my obligation and continue walking into the village? I passed a few yards, then heard a voice telling me to go home. After passing several yards I again encountered a few of these robbers. They stopped me, screamed at me and ordered me to go to the yard of Jakob Penner. I did so, followed by two of the killers. Then I heard someone begin to cry. It was Penner's son-in-law, Abraham Dyck. A shot and he fell dead. I was horrified, yet had to continue walking. The commander came out of the house and shouted: "You have already been in my custody once!" Again he commanded a soldier to take me to the street. I was one and a half versts from my quarters. An indescribable anxiety overwhelmed me. How I prayed to God to bring me safely home. If my time had come, I wished to die with my loved ones.

Every yard was filled with Makhnovites. There was shouting and swearing interspersed with the crying of the widows and orphans whose husbands and fathers had just been killed. God finally brought me safely to my family.

The seven Makhnovites who were spending the night with us ordered us to kill some chickens and make *borshch*. We did so since the food was to be prepared quickly.

The entire village was surrounded by cavalry. Guards were posted on all the yards, including ours. One of them frequently came into the room cursing and mocking. He said that all the Germans should be killed. When they had eaten I went into the bedroom to ready it for the bandits. How often I have thought of the words "Love your enemies, bless those who curse you." These men demanded our best beds and I prepared them as well as I could. Yet they did not go to sleep. I was in the front room when the guard came into the house and demanded a drink of water. When he had drunk he began to scream at me: "There is a fly in the water and it is in my throat!" He shouted and screamed still louder. I apologized and said that was not possible. Nothing calmed him down and he threatened to shoot me. Finally he relaxed and all seven went to sleep. My wife and my brothers Jakob and Klaas went into the living room. I took the Word of God, opened it and read a portion. In spite of our fear we calmed down.

I forget what portion we read. We all kneeled down and prayed that the Lord would deliver us from the power of darkness. I prayed first, then dear brother Jakob. He had just begun when there was a pounding on the locked door. We got up, took the lamp and opened the door. In walked the commander whom I had already met twice. At least twenty men followed him. We all went into my room. The commander immediately began to interrogate me. He asked who owned the property.

I said it was my brother Jakob. There were other questions—did I have land? Then they interrogated my brother Klaas. I came to his defense and they freed him because he possessed no property. Then it was brother Jakob's turn. Did he have land? He answered yes.

The commander shouted for him to remove his clothing. He grew pale for he knew death was imminent. There was shouting and mocking. One person took a guitar and the other a violin and they played a wild tune. They, in their bloodlust, were celebrating the death of a person. What happens to humankind when they give themselves over to Satan? This murder commission walked the length of the village, at times killing several people in the family, at times killing the entire family.

As brother Jakob took off his clothes the soldiers divided them among themselves. The commander ordered his men to take Jakob outside and give him twenty-five strokes. We were certain they would do more. I was cut to the heart. I did not notice but my brother Klaas later reported that Jakob had said goodnight.

I personally was in danger of death throughout the night. The commander ordered that the doors be locked and that we were not to leave. We went into the room but no one said a word for we were all agitated and depressed. Brother Jakob did not return. I told my dear wife that I would not hide, that if my time had come I would stay with my family. At least then they would know what had happened to me.

At twelve midnight one of the seven sleepers appeared and threatened with his rifle. He was in his night clothes and asked if brother Jakob had returned. After a few minutes he went back to the bedroom. I had to support my dear wife who was trembling severely. A few minutes later he reappeared and ordered breakfast for 5 AM. When my wife regained her composure she insisted we invite the Polish refugees in the nearby building to keep us company. Together with them we went to the chicken barn, killed some chickens and prepared a soup. At 4 AM there was knocking at the back door. Two drunken bandits entered. They chased out the refugees. "Since your landlord no longer lives you are the owner. Come and give us your murdered brother's money." I told them he had already given them everything. "Then your life is not worth any more than his," they screamed. I walked into the barn where I was to be shot.

He called me back and asked if I would now give him my brother's money. Suddenly he began to speak High German. I realized he was a [German] Catholic. He cursed and hit me on the head and asked whether I would give him money or forfeit my life. I finally gave him the money from my wife's butter sales. They divided the money among themselves, politely shook our hands and walked into the bedroom of the seven. They told me to get clean underclothes for these men, then left.

Later we learned that these two men had killed the village teachers and cut them in pieces. We prepared breakfast for our night guests who ate and seemed content. They didn't demand underclothes. Before they left they threatened to shoot me and take my wife with them, but the Eternal Helper rescued us.

Now Klaas, my wife and I went to look for Jakob. We found him dead on the manure pile. His head had been split open, his neck and right hand almost cut off. His body had been cut open. My heart still bleeds today when I think back. We went to our neighbours but they too had been killed. Some seventy-four persons lost their lives. The women and children were on the streets wailing and crying.

My wife and I decided to go to Nikolaipole (Village No. 1). As we left the village we went into a valley in order to steal away. Suddenly we were confronted by three riders who asked where we were going. I excused myself and requested permission to go to Nikolaipole, which they granted us. It was six versts and we were carrying our little Justina. There was deep mud and I asked my wife if she could go on. Fear drove us onward and we arrived safely at my brother-in-law's in Nikolaipole.

That was Sunday morning, October 27.

On Tuesday October 29 people drove from all the villages to collect and bury the bodies. I began at one end of the village and laid five bodies on the wagon. That was very difficult. Their heads had been shattered and we had to gather various body parts like hands and feet. That took courage and fortitude. How it pained us. It was like a battlefield. Some faces were so shattered as to be unrecognizable. All seventy-four bodies, seventy-one men and three women were taken to the cemetery. I am incapable of describing the scene. How sad it was to see the survivors. Some screamed, others prayed or hugged each other.

People worked hard, for evening was approaching. The graves were dug and the bodies placed in them. With God's help we managed to finish by evening. Then I returned to Nikolaipole. A number stayed in Eichenfeld (Village No. 4) and as a result ten more persons lost their lives, nine men and a woman who had been mentally ill for twenty years. The men had been in the village to look after the cattle which were bellowing for water. The men who survived fled.

We stayed in Nikolaipole. One day the bandits arrived there searching for people from Eichenfeld (Village No.4). They were known to us, Russians from a neighbouring village. When they saw me they threatened to shoot me.

The next morning we took a wagon and fled to Neuendorf, fifteen versts away from the village. There were thousands of Makhnovites there and we stayed only one week before returning to my brother-in-law's in Nikolaipole. We stayed there until spring and eventually decided to emigrate to Canada.

Notes

Taken from David A. Quiring, "Die Schreckenszeit in dem Dorfe Eichenfeld, Sued-Russland, im Oktober 1919," *Mennonitische Rundschau*, Vol. 49 (1926) nos. 34-41. Translated by John B. Toews.

Chapter 6
A Night of Horror,
as told by Two Sisters

Helena Harder Martens' Story

So it happened that on October 26, 1919 a thieving band of about 400 persons entered our village, and according to plan, immediately took up their quarters in homes and then began to rob clothing, valuables and food. In every house there were eight to twelve bandits [who] ordered everything imaginable to be prepared for them and served before them. But the head of the family had to taste every dish first.

In the evening the rampage began. One neighbour knew nothing of the next. Immediate death threatened anyone who would have tried to flee. The murderers construed a variety of atrocities. One father and his four sons had to beat each other with gun barrels, and for that they had to strip naked. Another neighbour had to go through the village searching for a Cossack riding whip, only to be killed with it later. And much more.

My father was beaten left and right until he lost consciousness and the strength to stand and so fell to the floor. Then the terrorists trampled on his head, chest and body until the floor was covered with his blood. On their command and with the help of mother, he stood to his feet, and accompanied by both [my] brothers they were driven outside, stripped, and with sabers butchered, bandit-style, near the straw stacks.

Women and even twelve-year-old girls were raped, manhandled in a variety of ways and infected with venereal diseases. I and my sisters (thanks be to God!) did not fall into these devilish hands.

That night a total of 72 persons, including three women, were murdered. Only in the morning of the next day, after the bloodthirsty had left the village, did the about 45 widows and 200 orphans start on their flight to relatives and acquaintances in the neighbouring Mennonite villages. The heart no longer was bound to the earthly possessions; no one knew whether he would even escape with his life from these atrocities. How easy it would have been for these, or another group of bandits, to overrun these women and children fleeing on foot.

And barely had those who fled left their homes when a number of the same rogues re-entered on foot and on horseback to begin with the plunder and destruction of the buildings. In 1921 during our teaching time in Nikolaipole, Peter and I visited the tragic home place of our youth, and everywhere found in place of the well-cared-for village surrounded by fruit trees only shrubs and ruins.

Those who survived that night first went to No. 3 Adelsheim/Dolinovka. I and my sister and mother found temporary lodging at my uncle Jacob Andres', who at the time was village school teacher in No. 2 Franzfeld/Varvarovka. Brother Jacob was attending school there at the time and thus was saved from the fate that befell the other brothers. We were at Andres' for two months. And then, because the typhus epidemic started and we as "have-nots" and refugees were without employment, we went to No. 3 to take care of the fellow sufferers from No. 4, to whom few dared draw near, until we too in turn became ill and found lodging at Jacob Bartsch's (God bless them!) where we received the best possible care under the circumstances. When convalescence began, although still bedridden, we were taken to Khortitsa to stay with Aunt Pauls who had invited us. On repeated invitation we changed our quarters for the fourth time and moved to Uncle Jacob Krahn's in Rosental. Soon afterwards the opportunity came to go for a longer period of time and a greater distance (100 miles) to brother-in-law Aron Funk's place in Steinfeld.

Katharina Harder Pätkau's Story

October 26, 1919. The day was dull and overcast. Already in the morning there was much uneasiness. Horse-back riders, wagons drawn by horses and loaded with heavily armed men, herds of stolen cattle, moved through the village. It was restless, very restless and fear filled the hearts of the villagers. About ten in the morning there was a very noisy disturbance and screaming in the yard of Heinrich Heinrichs. One shot rang out and the father lay dead. And very soon there was a heavy pounding on our locked door and someone demanded admittance. They demanded food, baked goods and lodging. There was no time to bake bread; they wanted it immediately. So one baking sheet of *Schnetke* after another was filled and baked. As they came hot out of the oven, dirty hands grabbed for it and in a moment the pan was empty. More! We couldn't keep up.

The day dragged into evening and the yard remained full of wagons and riders. As dusk was settling over the village a troop of Makhnovite bandits galloped through the village at full speed and set a guard at either end of the village so that no one could escape. The demand was for more food.

At the Harders', mother and the two daughters, Katharina and Helena, were in the kitchen when brother Peter came in, took the spoon out of Katharina's hand, and said, "Disappear!" The sisters fled through the back door, through the barn and into the chicken barn where they hid behind the door. But they were immediately followed. They were being hunted and yet as though blinded [the Makhnovites] passed by the door and didn't see the door or the girls. But it was not safe here, so they fled again, protected by the darkness through the orchard to a neighbour somewhat separated from the rest. But it was not safe here either, and again they fled to the end of the village to the Schmidts.

These were not landowners and therefore were not being attacked by the Mahhnovite bandits. They asked here for protection and the head of the house let them come in. With kerchiefs tied over their hair they tried to hide their faces as much as possible, and seated themselves among the daughters of the house. Only minutes later there was a loud pounding on the door and it was thrown wide open. There before them stood the same terror-instilling huge fellow, with knives dangling from his belt, that had been at their home. He screamed, "Are these all your girls?" But he was not satisfied with the answer and went around peering with piercing eyes into every face, and then left with the warning that if Mr. Schmidt was housing any of the daughters of the bourgeoisie it would cost his life.

Oh, how long was that night! Finally the morning began to dawn and the girls dared look toward their home. The shutters were closed. The wide village street was empty. They saw their mother walking all alone on the street. Where should she go? They ran to her. And then the gruesome tragedy of the night was revealed. Father and two brothers had been taken out during the night and had been hacked to death near the straw stacks—one by each of three stacks. The rain of the night had covered everything with slippery ice, but had also washed the wounds clean. Others had to take care of the bodies. The village was empty except for a few men on horseback.

There was nothing left but to flee. Through the mud on foot they went to the next village of Nikolaipole. The neighbour's wife was with them. She was carrying her child on her back the several miles. Others offered to carry it for her but she refused help. Some lost their shoes, but on they went.

A few days later Katharina, Helena and their brother Jacob, who at the time of the murders had been in another village, returned to their home to look around, but barely had they entered the house when horseback riders were there again and asked what they wanted. The girls disappeared. Jacob answered several questions. As soon as the rider left, they dared not look any more but left immediately, never to return.

Notes

Helena Harder Martens, "A Short Autobiography," and Katharina Harder Pätkau, "A Night of Terror," *A Family Album: Pätkau-Harder 1757-1980*, comp. and trans. Esther L. Pätkau (Saskatoon, 1980), 181-186.

Chapter 7
The Tent Missionaries
Abram Kröker

The following massacre occurred in October, 1919 in the German village of Eichenfeld/Dubovka (Novopetrovka) in the *guberniia* and *uezd* of Ekaterinoslav. [An eyewitness] writes:

After a blessed service during the summer in the north, we returned to our centre, the railway station Paniutina in the south, in order to prepare for further work. We approached the Ekaterinoslav region which had been overrun by Makhnovite troops while we were on our mission trip. Soon we were passing through the region occupied by military forces. We frequently had encounters with these soldiers who repeatedly disturbed our church services. Continuing our work, we reached the Mennonite settlement of Nikolaipole which comprised five villages. Here we decided to work and hold services for a longer time.

The inhabitants of these villages were in a state of agitation. Makhnovite bands had seized certain villages, robbing and abusing the inhabitants. God protected us in a wonderful way and we testified happily about our Lord. During the final days, brother Jacob Dyck was particularly filled with the spirit and testified with great strength at the gatherings.

On Friday, October 25, 1919, at 9:00 AM, after gathering for prayer in the home of a certain brother, we divided into three groups which would each work in a different village. agreeing to meet again the following Monday.

Jacob Dyck chose the village of Eichenfeld/Dubovka, where no private services had previously been held. The following accompanied brother Dyck: Iushkevich, Golitsyn, the local minister Johann Schellenberg, and the sisters Luise Hübert-Suckau and Regina Rosenberg, a converted Jew, all of whom stayed at the home of the widow Peters.

After several incidents, the Makhnovite authorities gave brother Dyck permission to hold tent meetings, the first being set for the afternoon of Saturday, 26 October, the last day of life of our beloved tent missionaries.

That morning, widow Peters was preparing breakfast for the missionaries when a number of Makhnovites entered and without a word sat down at the breakfast table. They urged the missionary brothers and sisters to take their places, making space for them at the table.

Jacob Dyck explained that his group of evangelical Christians did not eat until after their morning devotions. He therefore read a scripture passage, commented on what he had read, and invited everyone to stand for prayer. The Makhnovites did as they were told. After breakfast, however, the Makhnovites demanded that dance music be played, which the evangelical sisters refused to do, singing gospel songs instead. More Makhnovites entered the room until it was quite full, brother Dyck all the while preaching God's Word to them until his voice finally gave out around noon. Sister Peters immediately gave him two raw eggs whereupon he resumed his preaching.

When the marauders returned to their barracks at midday the sisters proceeded to the schoolhouse to hold a meeting with the children. Accompanied by the brothers Dyck and

Schellenberg, the missionaries spoke briefly to the school teachers, bending their knees in prayer. Several Makhnovites entered, abruptly demanding that brother Dyck produce papers authorizing such a meeting, which he did. At the same time he gave an eloquent testimony of his faith. The Makhnovites stood there, eyes downcast, scarcely able to conceal the dark intentions that filled their hearts. Then, uttering the cryptic words, "We know you well, you missionaries," they left the school house.

Other Makhnovites entered. They met brother Golitsyn, asking him who he was and when he replied that he was a preacher they began to beat him. As the brother lay there bleeding on the floor, they ordered sister Peters to produce clean cloth, picked up the brother, removed his blood-soaked clothes, dressed his wounds and ordered him to lead them to the schoolhouse where the other missionaries still were. As they entered the school, the Makhnovites ordered the evangelists to place themselves against the wall, which the brothers and sisters did. The teacher entered his classroom and begged the men not to commit their murders in the schoolroom.

The Makhnovites ordered the brothers and sisters to follow them to an empty barn across the street. They went to the opposite side of the street where there was an empty barn. As they were being led away, the wife of the school teacher looked through the window of another schoolroom and saw how the believers went there quite submissively. Jacob Dyck covered his face with his hands; then the two Makhnovites driving him forward hit him in the face with a bare sabre. As they entered the barn, a shot rang out. Sister Rosenberg emerged from the building, her eyes full of joy and while explaining something to them pointed heavenwards. The Makhnovites returned to the house where brother Iushkevitsch had stayed behind and soon returned with him to the barn.

While this bloody massacre was taking place in Eichenfeld/Dubovka, other Makhnovite bands were murdering inhabitants in other villages. Saturday evening it was our turn. The Makhnovites entered our meeting with the intention of shooting all of us. Brother Heinrich Epp (from Alexanderwohl) and I preached the Word and the Lord protected us in a wonderful way. Later, when we heard what had happened in Eichenfeld we proceeded there to check out the reports. Along the way we met a woman who with tear-filled eyes begged us not to continue our journey. All of its inhabitants had been killed, she said. She had witnessed the missionaries being murdered and had seen how one of the sisters had fallen to the ground still clutching her Bible.

Suddenly several Makhnovites sprang out of a farmyard and demanded to know where we were going. When I told them I had heard that several of our ministers had been murdered they exclaimed, "Aha—and you will be next!" One of them drew his sabre, demanding that I dismount and follow him into the farmyard. When I replied that I would stay where I was he ordered me to empty my pockets. I gave him my Bible and another book. When another of his comrades told him to leave me in peace another sister and I returned to our companions.

After two days, determined to find our murdered colleagues, we drove towards Eichenfeld/Dubovka where we met a man who said he would show us where they lay. At the first house in the village we found two mutilated bodies. At the other houses as well lay corpses in twos and threes with mutilated hands and faces. Finally we reached the barn where our brothers and sisters lay dead. We first happened across a body we could not identify. Then we found to the right two persons in their underclothes with their mutilated heads towards the door. They were Jacob Dyck and Golitsyn. At the door lay the body of Iushkevich, his face bent downwards in an attitude of prayer. His hand lay under his head and he had a deep wound in his neck. Further along we encountered the body of Regina Rosenberg, the converted Jew. It appeared that she too had been murdered while praying. She had two deep wounds in her neck and head. Not far from her lay sister Luise Hübert-Sukkau.

Notes

    Taken from Abram Kröker, *Bilder aus Sowjet-Russland* (Striegau in Schlesien, 1930), 13-19. Translated by Leona Gislason.

PART III
UKRAINIANS RECALL

Chapter 8
Oral History Interviews
Svetlana Bobyleva and Colleagues

"Not a single German home remained standing in the village," recalled 68-year-old Raisa Gurazda. "They were torn down. People travelling to Dneprostroi didn't want to pass through here. It was like a 'black hole,' deserted. The bricks were scattered around. It was desolate, and the cats slunk about, and the dogs."

She was speaking to Svetlana Bobyleva, Director of the Ukrainian-German Institute at Dniepropetrovsk National State University, Ukraine, leader of a three-person team that interviewed people in villages of the Nikolaipole district between April 27-29, 2001. The results, which appear abridged below, provide fresh insights into the Eichenfeld massacres and the manner in which memories of the event shaped the understanding of later generations of Ukrainians.

The Dnepropetrovsk team interviewed twenty-four people in seven villages. Thirteen had substantial memories of the disaster. All were elderly, and several of the oldest had vague first-hand memories of the events. Eighty-eight-year-old Luker'ia Tret'iak was six in 1919, and remembered the massacre because it happened on his cousin Cleopatra's wedding-day. Eighty-nine-year-old Iosif Moiseevich recalled how Makhno himself had stayed in his village. None, however, had been old enough in 1919 to recall events in detail. Their stories are second-hand, passed down from parents, older siblings, relatives and friends.

The accounts vary wildly on details. Raisa Gurazda heard that "they killed maybe 200, maybe 400." Fedor Starinets thought seventy-four men were killed, and perhaps "two or three women who tried to defend their husbands." Luker'ia Tret'iak did not know how many died, but thought the Makhnovites had murdered every Mennonite man in the village, and one woman. According to Grigorii Rezenko, "they massacred everyone. The entire village. Including the women and children." Fedor Starinets was more specific, confirming Mennonite reports that the Makhnovites singled out landowners as victims.

The respondents were more consistent in their explanations of the attack. Seven of the thirteen believed that Mennonite self-defense groups had provoked retaliation by firing on Makno's forces (a rumour often mentioned in Mennonite emigre sources). Fedor Starinets told his story in detail, concluding that "there was one German who said that they should arm themselves and fight back against the bandits. Some four Makhnovtsi were killed or wounded. Makhno himself had issued the order: 'Slaughter them all!'"

The respondents were also of one view in reporting looting after the massacres by Ukrainian peasants from neighbouring villages. Raisa Gurazda told how looters had prized Mennonite doors and windows in particular, while several recalled how villagers had even pilfered bricks from abandoned Mennonite homes.

This is, of course, a caricature of the complex and diverse Mennonite reality. Makhno himself recognized the divisions within Mennonite society when he singled out and murdered

An elderly Ukrainian villager brings flowers to the memorial.

only the landowners of Eichenfeld. But for those who carried out the attacks, the common identification of Mennonites as a privileged "German" minority must have helped them justify their actions. The survival today of such "us and them" distinctions is an important reminder of how vital is the task of re-incorporating the history of ethno-cultural and religious minorities into the mainstream of Ukrainian education and popular culture.

Interviews

Account of Raisa Pavlovna Gurazda (b. 1933), Village of Novo-Petrovka

The Ukrainians in Iazykova Village lived on the hill and were poor. Catherine the Great gave all the good land to the Germans.

Eichenfeld was a large village. In 1919 the Makhnovites fell upon it. They took everything—the chickens, the pigs—

and the people there put up some resistance. The fighting began, and the Eichenfelders killed two Makhnovites.

After a couple of days or a week the Makhnovites returned, and in the night they slaughtered all the men and even the little children—the boys. The victims weren't shot. Perhaps one was shot. They shot a woman who was defending her husband. She went crazy, tearing at her hair. The rest they killed with sabres or knives. I don't know exactly.

They killed the people in their homes. They went quietly from house to house and killed everyone, even the little boys. They killed maybe 200, maybe 400. I don't remember.

Two people escaped, one man and one boy, his son. They were in a wagon. They had gone somewhere and hadn't returned yet. Perhaps they heard some noise. Something put them on their guard, and they stayed away. I don't know their names.

The women buried the dead. Maybe someone helped them.

It was, I'm sure, in the fall. Certainly not in the winter.

Later some daring people from neighbouring villages came, after everything was deserted. They took all the doors and windows. The Germans had everything of the best quality, big two-story brick homes, fine wooden floors and ceilings. The wood was all painted.

All of the survivors went to the village of Fedorovka. Later they came here, by way of Dnieprostroi. A few came from Avgustinovka, but just a handful.

Not a single German home remained standing in the village, they were torn down. People travelling to Dnieprostroi didn't want to pass through here. It was like a "black hole," deserted. The bricks were scattered around. It was desolate, and the cats slunk about, and the dogs.

I've lived in this village since 1952. There were two Germans here who came from Dolinovka: Grigorii Iakovlevich Thiessen and someone named Wiebe. They had returned from Kazakhstan. Nobody took them away in 1941, they ran away on their own. They were very punctual people, cultured, clean—not "our people" . . . .

In our village there also lived a man named Cheredinchenko. He had a wife called "Prusachka." She talked with an accent. Her brother's wife came to stay with her from Kazakhstan. She [the brother's wife] was originally from Nikolaipole.

There was no hostility toward Germans in the local area. I remember that their villages were very beautiful. There were pear and apricot trees everywhere—all planted by the Germans. In Dolinovka there were two rows of wild pear trees. With us everything was run down, dishevelled, dirty. With them, everything was cultured.

Our people worked for the Germans as cooks, cleaners, and gardeners. The Germans kept pigs. They would render the fat, and they had lots of *salo* . . . .

Account of Fedor Nazarovich Starinets, (b. 1924), Village of Fedorovka

Around here there were German colonies. Here in the village of Fedorovka the soil was sandy, so the Germans didn't take it.

When the dam was built [at Dnieprostroi], Fedorovka was flooded. There used to be over 200 homes, but now there are just over 100. In Fedorovka there was a steam ship port. Forty-three steam ships docked here. There was a ferry here—it carried grain, and also Germans.

My father, Nazar Akimovich, was trained by a German as a joiner. After my father started working for that German, another German (maybe his brother) asked if he could take my father. The first German replied: "He's not altogether useless, take him."

My father worked in that German's house for a year, washing dishes, and then he was made an apprentice. When the Makhnovites wiped out Eichenfeld, that German survived, and afterwards he gave some of his tools to my father. Seventy-four people were killed with sabres, along with two or three women who tried to defend their husbands. But maybe [my father's employer] hid, I don't know. Those who survived were no longer permitted to live here. People from neighbouring villages not only took the belongings from the houses, they tore down the houses themselves. I don't remember the name of [my father's employer] who survived. He wasn't married. Among the tools was a wood plane. My mother remembered those events very well.

They were cut down at night. The Germans lived better, and they were being robbed. There was one German who said that it was necessary for them to arm themselves and repel the robbers. Something like four Makhnovites were killed or wounded. Makhno issued the order: "Slaughter them all!" But when evening came he said: "Don't harm the workers, women, or children." They went from house to house and cut them down. Maybe someone escaped.

After the killing, the Makhnovites went to Fedorovka to spend the night. They drew their sabres, and blood poured from the blades.

Who buried the dead, and how—I don't know.

During the Second World War, I had finished grade nine, and I was taken away to Germany. I was there three years. More than twenty of us young people were taken away to Germany. Only five survived. We worked in a sawmill. At first, they took the young, and later the old.

At the time of the war, there were German Ukrainians here. They collaborated at first. The police were our own people, Ukrainians.

Account of Luker'ia Aleksandrovich Tret'iak (b. 1913), Village of Nikolaipole

The Germans had one organizer. They didn't want to allow Makhno onto this side of the Dnieper, so they went up on the hill and began shooting at the Makhnovites. For that, they were cut down. Makhno didn't touch other German villages in the region, because they had remained quiet.

It was my cousin Cleopatra Smiezhko's wedding day. In the evening the Makhnovites left to go for a walk. They came back in the morning, covered in blood. They had gone to Eichenfeld.

My sister asked, "What's with the blood?"

"Why, we cut down all the Germans."

They went to the first house, got the homeowner, and took him with them to the next house. When the second homeowner opened his door, they killed the first homeowner. So they went, from house to house, through the whole village.

They killed only the men. And so they cut down the whole village, except the women, apart from one who tried to defend her husband. They killed her too. The murdered were all buried in one grave in the orchard.

The women and children fled to Dolinovka and Nikolaipole. The Funk children, Igor, David, Katya, and Ivan, were in Novo-Petrovka.

In 1919 the Makhnovites and some local people from Fedorovka attacked Eichenfeld. After the pogrom, people from Fedorovka robbed Eichenfeld. . . .

Account of Nadezhda Timofeevna Gurazda (b. 1914), Village of Pershe Travnia

My parents told me that the Germans were hardworking and orderly; even their six-year old boys worked side-by-side with their fathers. They ate according to a schedule. If you wanted to go to them to get a job, then the first thing they did was to sit you down to eat while they watched you. If you ate well and quickly, then you would work hard too. They paid decent wages, and they were honest about paying them. My parents went and planted potatoes for them. They were fed two or three times a day, and paid every evening. Sometimes my parents ate with them, and sometimes separately. It depended.

The Germans organized self-defence units, and when Makhno came, a few [of his men] were killed. Makhno rounded them up and slaughtered them all, young and old. Only a few were spared. How they were buried, I don't know, but I think it was in just a few mass graves. The Makhnovites were strong, and so they prevailed. In 1919 the women fled to Nikolaipole and other villages. Our people went to Eichenfeld and took the houses, the bricks. . . .

Account of Iosef Moiseevich Mikheenko (b. 1912), Village of Fedorovka

I was little then. I was six years old. I heard something about it. Makhno took forage (barley, etc.) from that village for our horses, our people. The Makhnovites stayed in our village.

There was talk that the people in Eichenfeld had guns. The Germans had heavy machine guns, and the Makhnovites only had small calibre guns, like .45's. When Makhno set out for Eichenfeld, the people there began to shoot their guns and machine guns. Then Makhno returned fire, and the Germans raised a white flag to show that they surrendered. The Makhnovites occupied their houses. Makhno issued an order to his commanders to kill all the males, from the youngest to the oldest. They killed them all, two dozen property owners. Cut them down, shot them. But some fled to the neighbouring colony. The village stood empty. And then, all who could went and took the cattle.

Then, during the construction of Dnieprostroi, people from Fedorovka and Avgustinovka settled there. My mother was born in Avgustinovka.

I personally saw Makhno in our village. His headquarters weren't in our home, but in a bigger, better home. He was small of stature and followed by a retinue to guard him. His politics were like this: if a household had three horses, then he took one. If it had two horses, then he didn't take any. Wherever the Makhnovites decided to stay, the people there had to feed them. The Makhnovites often stayed with us. Makhno often ranged throughout the Zaporizhzhia and Ekaterinoslav districts. Whatever the people had, the Makhnovites would use. They found out and knew everything that each household owned. Poor Ukrainians treated Makhno as a guest, and the rich treated him as an enemy.

Account of Vera Andreevna Ivaniuk (b. 1927), Village of Dolinovka.

My mother, Maria Fedorovna Gurazda, was born in Fedorovka. My father, Andrei Ivanovich Lysenko, was born in Bashmachka. He worked for Germans in Dolinovka, and met and married my mother here. My father showed me a German home near here, and I still remember it. Now there is a field there.

One house I remember; my father showed it to me. He worked there. The owner had three sons. If he was going somewhere, he would call my father in and say: "Andrei, now you are the master! Keep the boys in line." And when he would return, he would always bring back presents. He never insulted either my mother or my father. If a person worked, then he was appreciated. Then my parents married and moved to Bashmachka. But our relatives lived in Dolinovka, so we came to visit. . . .

I remember very well that it was beautiful here. The area was clean, and trees and columns lined the roads. There were ponds in the orchards, and we would go rowing. . . .

I remember that nearby was Eichenfeld. Mama and my father told me (in what year I don't remember) that they went to mow hay on Dnieprov Hill, where the Kurgan is, and from there they saw Makhno come along. People began to shoot from the village of Eichenfeld. That night Makhno went to Eichenfeld and killed all the males, even those who were still in their cradles. And the women fled where they could.

Where have their houses gone? Not one German house still stands there. And when the people of Fedorovka were uprooted because of the Dnieprostroi dam, they settled on the site and built homes.

How the victims were buried, I don't know. The women gradually left. The Makhnovites didn't harm them.

My mother's sister and other little girls went to Eichenfeld and found cradles for their dolls. I remember my aunt played with a cradle like that. . . .

Notes

This interview project in Ukrainian villages close to one-time Eichenfeld was conducted in spring 2001 by a team of researchers under the guidance of Svetlana Bobyleva, Director, Ukrainian-German Institute, National State University of Dnepropetrovsk. This introduction to the project, and the summary and translation of its findings has been prepared by John Staples, Department of History, State University of New York at Fredonia, USA.

Part IV
WORDS OF REFLECTION

Chapter 9
Those Evil Times
Fedor G. Turchenko
Speech delivered at memorial service in Novopetrovka, May 27, 2001

Honoured Guests, Colleagues, Fellow Citizens,

On this spring day when nature so generously celebrates life in all its colour, it is the memory of the dead that has brought us together at this time and place, a cemetery. We gather in memory of those whose lives were violently foreshortened—as victims of a bloody massacre which took place in this village in the autumn of 1919. The years 1917 to 1921 were a time of fierce inter-group struggles throughout the length and breadth of Ukraine. The civil war took away the lives of hundreds of thousands of people of different nationalities and beliefs—Ukrainians, Russians, Jews and members of all other nationalities who lived in Ukraine. Included among these victims were also Mennonites. From the second half of the nineteenth century they had lived peacefully in the Nikolaifeld/ Nikolaipole volost as models of hard work, of wise economic management, of entrepreneurship and of self-discipline. They had lived in peace with other residents of the region, in the first instance with Ukrainians with whom they had found a common understanding. Through joint efforts these groups had created a vital economic system which contributed to the economic development of the Zaporizhzhe area and to its emergence as a highly developed region of Ukraine.

Were there problems in this life? Of course there were. By the twentieth century the Tsarist regime had become an anachronism and was approaching its end. Life required the liquidation of the empire. People were striving towards national self-determination, all wanted freedom of expression, the freedom to speak their native languages and to teach their children in their own languages. Society was prepared to conduct its own political affairs and demanded the freedom to do so. The overwhelming majority of the population strove to achieve modernization and the Europeanization of its life. Everyone clamoured for change. When the Tsarist regime was liquidated and the Ukrainian revolution followed quickly in its wake, there began the rebirth of the nation state. It was a period in which the enthusiasm of society hardly knew bounds. But at that time, few people could foresee that the events which followed would be carried by a wave of unspeakable violence and inflict huge losses. These events were accompanied by a cynical disregard of generally accepted norms of human behaviour, a disregard which Ukraine had not known for centuries.

It was a time of unimaginable cruelty. And the victims of this often unmotivated and totally irrational cruelty were people who in many cases had tried to steer clear of the titanic political struggles of the civil war. This describes the conduct of those Mennonites who lie buried in this plot of ground.

More than eighty years have elapsed since that time. Two generations have passed from the scene. Ukraine has become independent. Mennonites were forced to leave the steppe lands of the Dnieper region. This departure represents for us, its present-day residents, a great loss. But having ourselves passed through the fire of Communist totalitarianism, we also remember those who organized and participated in the pogroms against Mennonite villages whose victims lie buried here. It pains us to realize that in this massacre, and in similar ones, people from this locality, our compatriots, participated actively. It gives us no pleasure to admit that at that time a part of our society was gripped by a frenzy of vengeance. But the victims of this vengeance, including our Mennonites, were guilty of nothing

It should be remembered, however, that the pogromists and killers did not act in the interest of Ukraine, they did not act in its name. In their strivings and wishes, which often did not exceed primitive feelings of vengeance and greed, they seized what was not theirs, including the lives of others. It is not by chance that these people stood against the independence of Ukraine, against the wishes of its people to live in their own democratic country. Directly or indirectly they also contributed to the establishment on this territory of the bloody Bolshevik dictatorship which destroyed the lives of millions in Ukraine, of different nationalities. The pogromists and killers created all of the essential psychological preconditions for the triumph of this regime.

Today all this lies in the past. At present, in spite of huge economic difficulties, peace and inter-ethnic accord have been preserved in Ukraine. We are sure that this will continue as well.

As we pass by this cemetery and remember that savage time with its innocent victims let us also look to the future. As history continues its flow let us remember the cruelties of the past in order that we may seek to prevent their repetition.

May they rest in peace!

Chapter 10
Let There Be Peace
John B. Toews
Homily Delivered at Eichenfeld Memorial Service,
May 27, 2001

On September 23, 1995, while searching for this Eichenfeld mass grave and others, we met Safron Tretyak here in Novopetrovka. Thanks to the kindness and skill of interpreter Liudmila Kariaka he recounted for us the events of that tragic night in 1919. He wasn't sure why it happened—he was only seventeen at the time—but he felt it should not have happened. In his words "they were good people." He had worked for them and remembered some of their names—von Kampen, Friesen and Dyck.

Two months ago (March 27) in Vancouver, Canada, I sat with a Mr. Jakob Dyck. He is ninety-four years of age. On that fateful October night he was a thirteen-year-old lad. How vividly he recalled the experiences of that night—the soldiers, the violence, the stabbings, the shootings—and the execution of his father. At that point his eyes filled with tears—and he is a man of great self-control—and he said: "I can still see it all, as though it was yesterday."

Here was violence in the midst of a civil war which engulfed this vast and beautiful land. Here was one incidence of violence among many. Today we stand here to commemorate those who perished and to say no to violence—violence which is so much a part of every war.

War never solves problems. In our country we have a television station called the History Channel. Part of its program relates to playing film footage of WWII. Somehow as you see ships sunk, airplanes shot down, tanks and equipment destroyed and humans killed you are to believe that this is glorious, heroic, that it proves the rightness of our cause. The other side of the story is rarely told:

Families who have to survive without fathers;

Victims, both soldiers and civilians, who spend a lifetime as cripples, forgotten by society;

Individuals who are mentally and spiritually broken by the horrors of war;

And the lingering hatred on the part of both the victors and the vanquished.

Here in Novopetrovka we are commemorating one of the many tragedies in a civil war in which brother fought brother and brother killed brother.

And what of the famine and disease which followed in the wake of that conflict?

What of the mass starvation which stalked this land in the early 1930s?

What of the Nazi presence in Ukraine in the early 1940s with its mass destruction of cities and villages?

What of the long years of recovery characterized by hardship and sacrifice?

When we reflect on what happened here in 1919 or the many tragic events which have afflicted this land since then, it is easy to be angry and unforgiving. But where does that lead? Think of what recently happened in the countries west of you. In my home city of Vancouver we have many refugees from that region. What sad stories they tell:

Croatians fleeing from vengeful Serbians;
Serbians fleeing from vengeful Croatians;
Albanians fleeing from Kosovo;
Macedonians afraid of Albanians;

Friends, as long as we blame the other persons, list their many faults and wrong actions, as long as we continue to cry for revenge, nothing changes. The cycle of violence continues generation after generation. Civil conflicts raging throughout the world provide ample proof of this.

We here today are only a small group of people come to hold a memorial for people who never had one. In the older Mennonite tradition a person often died at home. It was customary to wash the body, dress it for burial, bring it into the home one last time, and then in solemn procession transport it to the church. There, through Bible reading, song and sermon, the community found comfort. If the cemetery was close at hand the entire community walked behind the coffin, often singing, to the open grave. More prayers were spoken, more songs sung. Slowly the coffin was lowered into the grave. Then as the community watched, the grave was filled with earth, often amid many tears. The funeral was followed by a common meal.

The people buried here were not washed or dressed for burial. There was no solemn procession to the church, no Bible reading or song, no march to the open grave, no coffin to lower, and little shedding of tears. It was a burial amid heartbreak, fear and uncertainty where, as one report has it, "widows and orphans walked about like shadows." Instead of a funeral meal the survivors fled.

John B. Toews speaks at the memorial ceremony. Larissa Goryacheva (Intourist Zaporizhe) translates while Steve Shirk (MCC for the former Soviet Union) observes.

In the Mennonite Christian tradition, as is true in the Catholic and Orthodox Christian practice, it is important for the community or representatives of the community to commit the body to the earth. We have come to do that and are thankful that people from Novopetrovka and elsewhere have come to mourn with us. It is true that most of us can no longer speak to you in your language and that most of you cannot speak to us in ours. The important thing is that we stand here together.

We want to say to one another that there is a better way than violence.

We want to say that no person is less a human being because of colour, language, nationality or belief.

We want to say that we are all created in the image of God. In the name of Christ whom Mennonites, Orthodox and Baptists honor we want to speak words of love and peace to one another.

At this site of twelve mass graves holding the remains of more than 80 people we want to speak of forgiveness and reconciliation and future friendship.

We also want to speak of our faith in another time and another life which follows death.

Long ago in an ancient land and in an ancient tongue a person known to us only as Job asked a difficult question. It is recorded for us in the Christian Scriptures: "If a person dies shall he live again?" (Job 14:14). Whatever our culture, language or beliefs this question confronts us whenever we stand in the presence of death. When we think of the people buried here we can come to only one conclusion. In the end death is the only sure thing in life. The statistic never changes: one out of one dies.

The Christian Scriptures tell us that in yet a different land, at a different time and in a different language Jesus of Nazareth is comforting two sisters who have lost their brother Lazarus:

> I am the resurrection and the life. He who believes in me will live even though he dies and whoever lives and believes in me will never die (John 11:25-26).

We have just passed the Easter season which the Orthodox tradition celebrates so marvelously. And of course it centres upon a group of disciples who had begun to believe that Jesus could conquer death, only to see him crucified by the Romans in a most cruel fashion. Death had struck at the very object of their faith. They had hoped for the death of death and nothing happened—only another death. But was that really the case?

When you read the Gospel texts concerning that first Easter morning they portray such excitement. There is confusion, a running to and from the tomb. People reported seeing the dead person alive, the very people who had witnessed his execution. Soon the evidence was overwhelming—the disciples saw the dead person alive in their very midst. Soon they were celebrating the death of death because they saw the risen Christ. You say it so well with your Easter greeting—"Christ is risen. He is risen indeed!"

And so though we mourn the killings of long ago, though we say they were unjust and unwarranted—the fact remains that the Mennonite victims buried here believed in the risen Christ and his promise of life everlasting. And so as we stand by this graveside we repeat once more the words of the Gospel often read at Mennonite graveside services:

> I am the resurrection and the life. He who believes in me will live even though he dies.

Part V
IN MEMORIAM

Chapter 11
Mennonite Victims of Civil War Murders and Massacres in the Nikolaipole Volost 1918-1920

In the Village of Eichenfeld/Dubovka (now Novopetrovka)

Seventy-six men and six women

On the night of Saturday to Sunday, October 26 to October 27, 1919, 70 men and 5 women were massacred in Eichenfeld, a small Mennonite village of around 300 persons, by a troop of some 400 men on horseback and in wagons. They were part of a much larger cavalry force in the area at the time under the leadership of Nestor Makhno. Two days later, on Tuesday, October 29, 1919, the victims were buried in eleven hastily-dug graves in the village cemetery. There was no funeral service.

In the ten days after the massacre of October 26-27, a further six men and one woman were killed in Eichenfeld, making a total of 82 massacre victims. They were buried in a further grave, number 12.

Grave One

1. Aaron David Klassen, 47 - minister
2. Aaron Aaron Klassen, 23 - son of #1
3. Johann Wilhelm Dyck, 35, son-in-law of #1
4. Johann Jacob Braun, nephew of #3

Grave Two

5. Wilhelm Martin Harder, 57
6. Heinrich Wilhelm Harder, 21 - son of #5

7. Peter Wilhelm Harder, 30 - son of #5
8. David David Woelk, 39
9. Isaak Wilhelm Guenther, 20 - from Gerhardstal
10. Heinrich Wilhelm Guenther, 18 - brother of #9
11. Isaak Isaak Guenther, 53 - father of #46 and #80
12. Cornelius F. Krause, 34 - from Kronsweide

Grave Three

13. Paul Gerhard Friesen, 34 -from Paulsheim
14. Katharina Friesen, nee Pauls, 33 - wife of #13
15. Abram Heinrich van Kampen, 26 - brother-in-law of #16, #18, #20 and, #22
16. Franz Johann Warkentin, 34 - brother of #18, #20 and #22
17. Susanna Warkentin, nee Redekopp, 34 - wife of #16 and daughter of #36
18. Isaak Johann Warkentin, 42 - son-in-law of #31
19. Johann Isaak Warkentin, 18 - son of # 18
20. Johann Johann Warkentin, 49 - brother of # 16, #18 and #22
21. David Johann Warkentin, 20 - son of #20
22. Daniel Johann Warkentin, 47 (?)
23. Daniel Daniel Warkentin, 22 - son of #22

Grave Four

24. Jacob J. Huebert, 64
25. Anna (Mrs. Daniel) Huebert, 40 - daughter-in-law of #24
26. Heinnch Kornelius Heinrichs, 42
27. Peter Abram Quiring, 43 - single, brother of #28 and #29

28. Jacob Abram Quiring, 38 - single
29. Johann Abram Quiring, 37
30. Johann Johann Epp, 48 - from Kronsweide, son-in-law of #31
31. Johann Jakob van Kampen, 70 - father of #32, #33 and #41
32. Jacob Johann van Kampen, 29, son of #31
33. Johann Johann van Kampen, 35, son of #31
34. Heinrich Abram Wiens, 42 - teacher
35. Wilhelm Paul Peters, 20 - teacher

Grave Five

36. David Wilhelm Redekopp, 76 - father-in-law of #16 and #22
37. Jacob Peter Wiebe, 42 - son-in-law of #36
38. Julius Jacob Lehn, 65 - single, refugee from Khortitsa settlement village of Neuenburg
39. Franz David Klassen, 46
40. Franz Franz Peters, 26 - single
41. David Johann van Kampen, 27 - brother-in-law of #42 to #45
42. Peter Johann Peters, 18 - brother of #43, #44 and #45
43. Daniel Johann Peters, 17
44. Franz Johann Peters, 20 - single
45. Kornelius Johann Peters, 22 - single
46. David Isaak Guenther, 32 - brother-in-law of #42-#45

Grave Six

47. Heinrich Jacob Dyck, 30 - from Gerhardstal
48. Abram Abram Dyck, 33 - son-in-law of #34

49. Abram Peter Heinrichs, 30
50. Peter ?, a student living with the Heinrichs family
51. Jacob Dombrovsky - son-in-law of #52
52. Abram Abram Teichroeb, 69
53. Jacob Abram Teichroeb, 47 - son of #52
54. Johann Johann Penner, 59 - father of #55-#58
55. Peter Johann Penner, 17
56. Johann Johann Penner, 19
57. Jacob Johann Penner, 23 - single
58. Franz Johann Penner, 34 - single

Grave Seven

59. Wilhelm Peter Klassen, 23 - son of #60
60. Peter Wilhelm Klassen, 56
61. Franz J. Bergen, 20 - son-in-law of #60, from Khortitsa settlement village of Neuhorst
62. Peter Wilhelm Pauls, 48 - single, son of #78
63. Kornelius Kornelius Pauls, 39

Grave Eight

The group of six tent missionaries, listed below, four men and two women, were of diverse ethnic backgrounds. They were killed with sabres in the granary of a certain Isaac Warkentin, #18 above.

64. Jacob J. Dyck, 30 - from the Molochna Mennonite settlement village of Halbstadt
65. Oskar Iushkevich - a Russian from Riga
66. J. Golitsyn - a Russian from Mogilev
67. Regina Rosenberg - a converted Jew from Konotop

68. Liese A. Huebert, 26 - from the Molochna Mennonite settlement village of Ruekenau
69. Johann Schellenberg, 54 - minister, buried on the nearby estate of Reinfeld, his home

Grave Nine

70. Jacob J. Regier, 54
71. Wilhelm Jacob Loewen, 18 - son of #70
72. Gerhard Johann Funk, 43

Grave Ten

73. Peter Jacob Block, 57 - father of #81

Grave Eleven

74. Heinrich David Hildebrand, 59
75. David Heinrich Hildebrand, 17 - son of #74

Grave Twelve

76. Jacob Kornelius Friesen, 78 - on November 2, with #77
77. David Gerhard Friesen, 22 - from Paulsheim, brother of # 13
78. Wilhelm Kornelius Pauls, 76 - on November 4, with #79 and #80
79. Kornelius Wilhelm Pauls, 42 - son of #78
80. Abram Isaak Guenther, 20 - son of #11
81. Johann Peter Block, 20 - son of #73, on November 6, with #82
82. Anna Huebert, wife of #24

Also buried in this grave is the body of Peter Abram Giesbrecht. Overcome by anguish, he committed suicide on October 31.

From the Village of Adelsheim/Dolinovka

Seven men
83. Kornelius Bergen
84. Heinrich Heinrich Janzen
85. Heinnch Kornelius Janzen
86. Abram Pankratz
87. Peter Warkentin
88. Kornelius Peter Willms
89. Gerhard Woelk

From the Village of Franzfeld/Varvarovka

Eleven men
90. Peter Isaak Friesen, 38
91. Heinrich Kornelius Janzen
92. Heinrich Heinrich Janzen
93. Jakob Jakob Neufeld, 56
94. Isaak Jakob Neufeld, 25
95. Abram Pankratz
96. Abram Heinrich Peters, 24
97. Abram Jakob Quiring, 52
98. Heinrich Heinrich Peters, 58
99. Jakob Jakob Quiring, 52
100. Gerhard David Redekopp, 38

From the Hamlet of Gerhardstal

Three men and one woman
101. Jakob Johann Braun, 35
102. Johann D. Hildebrand, 37
103. Johann Wilheim Klassen, 49
104. Katharina, nee Wiebe, Braun, 22

Names of the Dead

From the Village of Hochfeld/Morozovka

Thirteen men and three women

105. Widow Mrs. Peter Dyck, 54
106. Peter Peter Dyck, 25, son of #1
107. Wilhelm Peter Dyck, 21, son of #1
108. Kornelius Peter Epp, 60
109. Abram Abram Froese, 63
110. Kornelius Krahn, 29
111. Aron Kornelius Lehn, 68
112. Kornelius Kornelius Lehn, 71, Preacher
113. Peter Isaak Lehn, 25
114. Heinrich Johann Neustaedter, 42
115. Maria Heinrich Neustaedter, 15
116. Isaak Dietrich Rempel, 18
117. Johann Johann Thiessen, 56
118. Elisabeth Thiessen, 51, wife of #13
119. Johann Johann Winter, 35
120. Johann Johann Winter, 14, son of #15

In the Village Of Nikolaifeld/Nikolaipole

Four men

121. Johann Dietrich Huebert, 29
122. Johann Isaak Klassen, 56
123. Daniel Franz Peters, 55
124. Franz Franz Unrau, 22

From the Hamlet of Paulsheim

Three men

125. David Daniel Peters
126. Heinrich Jakob Peters, 16
127. Jakob Jakob Peters, 25

In the Hamlet of Petersdorf/Petrishevka

Nine men

128. Peter Janzen, teacher
129. Unnamed male refugee
130. Franz Daniel Peters, 76
131. Heinrich Kornelius Peters, 21
132. Johann Johann Peters, 32
133. Johann Johann Peters, 55
134. Kornelius Franz Peters, 32
135. Abram Abram Regier, 28, had fled from Kronsweide
136. Abram Regier, 60, had fled from Kronsweide

Notes

We gratefully acknowledge the help of Dr. Peter Letkemann, Winnipeg, on whose meticulous and devoted research the above lists are based.

Chapter 12
Memorial Stone

English translation of wording for memorial dedicated on Sunday, May 27, 2001, at Novopetrovka (onetime Eichenfeld/Dubovka) village cemetery for 136 Mennonite victims of civil war murders and massacres in the Nikolaipole Volost, 1918 to 1920.

In Sorrowful Remembrance
of Mennonite Victims of Civil War Murders and Massacres
in the Nikolaipole Volost, 1918-1920
Eichenfeld/Dubovka
on the night of 26-27 October 1919, and the following days,
seventy-six men and six women,
all but one buried in twelve nearby graves
Hochfeld/Morozovka
thirteen men and three women
Franzfeld/Varvarovka
eleven men
Petersdorf
nine men
And elsewhere in the Volost, 1918-1920
seventeen men and one woman
They will beat their swords into ploughshares and
their spears into pruning hooks
Isaiah 2:4
Erected in a spirit of reconciliation
by relatives of victims and friends of the Mennonite story

Chapter 13
Memorial Program
May 27, 2001

For Mennonite Victims of Civil War Murders and Massacres
In the Nikolaifeld/Nikolaipole Volost
Village of Eichenfeld/Dubovka (Novopetrovka)
May 27, 2001 - 3:00-5:00 pm

Opening Words and Unveiling of Monument

Introduction, Steven Shirk, Mennonite Central Committee, Chairman.

Welcome from Boris Letkemann, Chair, Zaporozhe Mennonite Church Board.

Greetings from Vladimir N. Pankin, Chair of Zaporozhe Raion Council.

Greetings from Jacob A. Plakhtyria, Chair of Nikolaipole Village Council.

Unveiling of memorial and reading of inscription.

"Symbolism of memorial," Anne Konrad Dyck reading words of designer Paul Epp.

"Time and place," Mikhail M. Sidorenko, Vice-Chair, Regional Committee for Historical Monuments.

Prayer.

Hymm: "Ich bete an die Macht der Liebe."

Reflections and Prayers

"An Evil Time," F. G. Turchenko, Dean, Faculty of History, University of Zaporizhzhe. "Sorrowful Remembrance,"
Vasili S. Kalyn, Ukrainian Orthodox priest.

Russian-language hymn, Zaporizhzhe Mennonite Church.

Prayer.

Naming Names and Seeking Peace
Reading of names of massacre victims.
Prayer on behalf of family members of victims.
"Let there be Peace," John B. Toews, Vancouver.
Hymn: "Die Gnade sei mit allen," verses 1, 2, 5.
Laying of flowers at monument.
Hymn: "So nimm denn meine Haende."

After Official Ceremony
Refreshments.
Retracing flight of Eichenfeld widows and children to the village of Adelsheim/Dolinovka.

About Pandora Press

Pandora Press is a small, independently owned press dedicated to making available modestly priced books that deal with Anabaptist, Mennonite, and Believers Church topics, both historical and theological. We welcome comments from our readers.

Visit our full-service online Bookstore:
www.pandorapress.com

John Howard Yoder, A*nabaptism and Reformation in Switzerland: An Historical and Theological Analysis of the Dialogues Between Anabaptists and Reformers* Anabaptist and Mennonite Studies Series (Kitchener: Pandora Press, 2004) Softcover, 509 pp., includes bibliography and indices. ISBN 1-894710-44-4 ISSN 1494-4081

Antje Jackelén, *The Dialogue Between Religion and Science: Challenges and Future Directions* (Kitchener: Pandora Press, 2004) Softcover, 143 pp., includes index. ISBN 1-894710-45-2

Ivan J. Kauffman, ed., *Just Policing: Mennonite-Catholic Theological Colloquium 2001-2002* The Bridgefolk Series (Kitchener: Pandora Press, 2004). Softcover, 127 pp., ISBN 1-894710-48-7.

Gerald W. Schlabach, ed., *On Baptism: Mennonite-Catholic Theological Colloquium 2001-2002* The Bridgefolk Series (Kitchener: Pandora Press, 2004). Softcover, 147 pp., ISBN 1-894710-47-9 ISSN 1711-9480.

Harvey L. Dyck, John R. Staples and John B. Toews, comp., trans. and ed. *Nestor Makhno and the Eichenfeld Massacre: A Civil War Tragedy in a Ukrainian Mennonite Village* (Kitchener: Pandora Press, 2004). Softcover, 115pp. ISBN 1-894710-46-0.

Jeffrey Wayne Taylor, *The Formation of the Primitive Baptist Movement* Studies in the Believers Church Tradition (Kitchener: Pandora Press, 2004). Softcover, 225 pp., includes bibliography and index. ISBN 1-894710-42-8 ISSN 1480-7432.

James C. Juhnke and Carol M. Hunter, *The Missing Peace: The Search for Nonviolent Alternatives in United States History* Second Expanded Edition (Kitchener: Pandora Press, 2004; co-published with Herald Press.) Softcover, 339 pp., includes index. ISBN 1-894710-46-3

Louise Hawkley and James C. Juhnke, eds., *Nonviolent America: History through the Eyes of Peace* Wedel Series 5 (North Newton: Bethel College, 2004, co-published with Pandora Press) Softcover, 269 pp., includes index. ISBN 1-889239-02-X

Karl Koop, *Anabaptist-Mennonite Confessions of Faith: the Development of a Tradition* (Kitchener: Pandora Press, 2004; co-published with Herald Press) Softcover, 178 pp., includes index. ISBN 1-894710-32-0

Lucille Marr, *The Transforming Power of a Century: Mennonite Central Committee and its Evolution in Ontario* (Kitchener: Pandora Press, 2003). Softcover, 390 pp., includes bibliography and index, ISBN 1-894710-41-x.

Erica Janzen, *Six Sugar Beets, Five Bitter Years* (Kitchener: Pandora Press, 2003). Softcover, 186 pp., ISBN 1-894710-37-1.

T. D. Regehr, *Faith Life and Witness in the Northwest, 1903-2003: Centenninal History of the Northwest Mennonite Conference* (Kitchener: Pandora Press, 2003). Softcover, 524 pp., includes index, ISBN 1-894710-39-8.

John A. Lapp and C. Arnold Snyder, gen.eds., *A Global Mennonite History. Volume One: Africa* (Kitchener: Pandora Press, 2003). Softcover, 320 pp., includes indexes, ISBN 1-894710-38-x.

George F. R. Ellis, *A Universe of Ethics Morality and Hope: Proceedings from the Second Annual Goshen Conference on Religion and Science* (Kitchener: Pandora Press, 2003; co-published with Herald Press.) Softcover, 148 pp. ISBN 1-894710-36-3

Donald Martin, *Old Order Mennonites of Ontario: Gelassenheit, Discipleship, Brotherhood* (Kitchener: Pandora Press, 2003; co-published with Herald Press.) Softcover, 381 pp., includes index. ISBN 1-894710-33-9

Mary A. Schiedel, *Pioneers in Ministry: Women Pastors in Ontario Mennonite Churches, 1973-2003* (Kitchener: Pandora Press, 2003) Softcover, 204 pp., ISBN 1-894710-35-5

Harry Loewen, ed., *Shepherds, Servants and Prophets* (Kitchener: Pandora Press, 2003; co-published with Herald Press) Softcover, 446 pp., ISBN 1-894710-35-5

Robert A. Riall, trans., Galen A. Peters, ed., *The Earliest Hymns of the Ausbund: Some Beautiful Christian Songs Composed and Sung in the Prison at Passau, Published 1564* (Kitchener: Pandora Press, 2003; co-published with Herald Press) Softcover, 468 pp., includes bibliography and index. ISBN 1-894710-34-7.

John A. Harder, *From Kleefeld With Love* (Kitchener: Pandora Press, 2003; co-published with Herald Press) Softcover, 198 pp. ISBN 1-894710-28-2

John F. Peters, *The Plain People: A Glimpse at Life Among the Old Order Mennonites of Ontario* (Kitchener: Pandora Press, 2003; co-published with Herald Press) Softcover, 54 pp. ISBN 1-894710-26-6

Robert S. Kreider, *My Early Years: An Autobiography* (Kitchener: Pandora Press, 2002; co-published with Herald Press) Softcover, 600 pp., index ISBN 1-894710-23-1

Helen Martens, *Hutterite Songs* (Kitchener: Pandora Press, 2002; co-published with Herald Press) Softcover, xxii, 328 pp. ISBN 1-894710-24-X

C. Arnold Snyder and Galen A. Peters, eds., *Reading the Anabaptist Bible: Reflections for Every Day of the Year* introduction by Arthur Paul Boers (Kitchener: Pandora Press, 2002; co-published with Herald Press.) Softcover, 415 pp. ISBN 1-894710-25-8

C. Arnold Snyder, ed., *Commoners and Community: Essays in Honour of Werner O. Packull* (Kitchener: Pandora Press, 2002; co-published with Herald Press.) Softcover, 324 pp. ISBN 1-894710-27-4

James O. Lehman, *Mennonite Tent Revivals: Howard Hammer and Myron Augsburger, 1952-1962* (Kitchener: Pandora Press, 2002; co-published with Herald Press) Softcover, xxiv, 318 pp. ISBN 1-894710-22-3

Lawrence Klippenstein and Jacob Dick, *Mennonite Alternative Service in Russia* (Kitchener: Pandora Press, 2002; co-published with Herald Press) Softcover, viii, 163 pp. ISBN 1-894710-21-5

Nancey Murphy, *Religion and Science* (Kitchener: Pandora Press, 2002; co-published with Herald Press) Softcover, 126 pp. ISBN 1-894710-20-7

Biblical Concordance of the Swiss Brethren, 1540. Trans. Gilbert Fast and Galen Peters; bib. intro. Joe Springer; ed. C. Arnold Snyder (Kitchener: Pandora Press, 2001; co-published with Herald Press) Softcover, lv, 227pp. ISBN 1-894710-16-9

Orland Gingerich, *The Amish of Canada* (Kitchener: Pandora Press, 2001; co-published with Herald Press.) Softcover, 244 pp., includes index. ISBN 1-894710-19-3

M. Darrol Bryant, *Religion in a New Key* (Kitchener: Pandora Press, 2001) Softcover, 136 pp., includes bib. refs. ISBN 1-894710- 18-5

Trans. Walter Klaassen, Frank Friesen, Werner O. Packull, ed. C. Arnold Snyder, *Sources of South German/Austrian Anabaptism* (Kitchener: Pandora Press, 2001; co-published with Herald Press.) Softcover, 430 pp. includes indexes. ISBN 1-894710-15-0

Pedro A. Sandín Fremaint y Pablo A. Jimémez, *Palabras Duras: Homilías* (Kitchener: Pandora Press, 2001). Softcover, 121 pp., ISBN 1-894710-17-7

Ruth Elizabeth Mooney, *Manual Para Crear Materiales de Educación Cristiana* (Kitchener: Pandora Press, 2001). Softcover, 206 pp., ISBN 1-894710-12-6

Esther and Malcolm Wenger, poetry by Ann Wenger, *Healing the Wounds* (Kitchener: Pandora Press, 2001; co-pub. with Herald Press). Softcover, 210 pp. ISBN 1-894710-09-6.

Otto H. Selles and Geraldine Selles-Ysselstein, *New Songs* (Kitchener: Pandora Press, 2001). Poetry and relief prints, 90pp. ISBN 1-894719-14-2

Pedro A. Sandín Fremaint, *Cuentos y Encuentros: Hacia una Educación Transformadora* (Kitchener: Pandora Press, 2001). Softcover 163 pp ISBN 1-894710-08-8.

A. James Reimer, *Mennonites and Classical Theology: Dogmatic Foundations for Christian Ethics* (Kitchener: Pandora Press, 2001; co-published with Herald Press) Softcover, 650pp. ISBN 0-9685543-7-7

Walter Klaassen, *Anabaptism: Neither Catholic nor Protestant*, 3rd ed (Kitchener: Pandora Press, 2001; co-pub. Herald Press) Softcover, 122pp. ISBN 1-894710-01-0

Dale Schrag & James Juhnke, eds., *Anabaptist Visions for the new Millennium: A search for identity* (Kitchener: Pandora Press, 2000; co-published with Herald Press) Softcover, 242 pp. ISBN 1-894710-00-2

Harry Loewen, ed., *Road to Freedom: Mennonites Escape the Land of Suffering* (Kitchener: Pandora Press, 2000; co-published with Herald Press) Hardcover, large format, 302pp. ISBN 0-9685543-5-0

Alan Kreider and Stuart Murray, eds., *Coming Home: Stories of Anabaptists in Britain and Ireland* (Kitchener: Pandora Press, 2000; co-published with Herald Press) Softcover, 220pp. ISBN 0-9685543-6-9

Edna Schroeder Thiessen and Angela Showalter, *A Life Displaced: A Mennonite Woman's Flight from War-Torn Poland* (Kitchener: Pandora Press, 2000; co-published with Herald Press) Softcover, xii, 218pp. ISBN 0-9685543-2-6

Stuart Murray, *Biblical Interpretation in the Anabaptist Tradition,* Studies in the Believers Tradition (Kitchener: Pandora Press, 2000; co-published with Herald Press) Softcover, 310pp. ISBN 0-9685543-3-4 ISSN 1480-7432.

Loren L. Johns, ed. *Apocalypticism and Millennialism,* Studies in the Believers Church Tradition (Kitchener: Pandora Press, 2000; co-published with Herald Press) Softcover, 419pp; Scripture and name indeces ISBN 0-9683462-9-4 ISSN 1480-7432

Later Writings by Pilgram Marpeck and his Circle. Volume 1: The Exposé, A Dialogue and Marpeck's Response to Caspar Schwenckfeld. Trans. Walter Klaassen, Werner Packull, and John Rempel (Kitchener: Pandora Press, 1999; co-published with Herald Press) Softcover, 157pp. ISBN 0-9683462-6-X

John Driver, *Radical Faith. An Alternative History of the Christian Church,* edited by Carrie Snyder. Kitchener: Pandora Press, 1999; co-published with Herald Press) Softcover, 334pp. ISBN 0-9683462-8-6

C. Arnold Snyder, *From Anabaptist Seed. The Historical Core of Anabaptist-Related Identity* (Kitchener: Pandora Press, 1999; co-published with Herald Press) Softcover, 53pp.; discussion questions. ISBN 0-9685543-0-X
Also available in Spanish translation: *De Semilla Anabautista,* from Pandora Press only.

John D. Thiesen, *Mennonite and Nazi? Attitudes Among Mennonite Colonists in Latin America, 1933-1945* (Kitchener: Pandora Press, 1999; co-published with Herald Press) Softcover, 330pp., 2 maps, 24 b/w illustrations, bibliography, index. ISBN 0-9683462-5-1

Lifting the Veil, a translation of *Aus meinem Leben: Erinnerungen von J.H. Janzen.* Ed. by Leonard Friesen; trans. by Walter Klaassen (Kitchener: Pandora Press, 1998; co-pub. with Herald Press). Softcover, 128pp.; 4pp. of illustrations. ISBN 0-9683462-1-9

Leonard Gross, *The Golden Years of the Hutterites,* rev. ed. (Kitchener: Pandora Press, 1998; co-pub. with Herald Press). Softcover, 280pp., index. ISBN 0-9683462-3-5

William H. Brackney, ed., *The Believers Church: A Voluntary Church,* Studies in the Believers Church Tradition (Kitchener: Pandora Press, 1998; co-published with Herald Press). Softcover, viii, 237pp., index. ISBN 0-9683462-0-0 ISSN 1480-7432.

An Annotated Hutterite Bibliography, compiled by Maria H. Krisztinkovich, ed. by Peter C. Erb (Kitchener: Pandora Press, 1998). (Ca. 2,700 entries) 312pp., cerlox bound, electronic, or both. ISBN (paper) 0-9698762-8-9/(disk) 0-9698762-9-7

Jacobus ten Doornkaat Koolman, *Dirk Philips. Friend and Colleague of Menno Simons*, trans. W. E. Keeney, ed. C. A. Snyder (Kitchener: Pandora Press, 1998; co-published with Herald Press). Softcover, xviii, 236pp., index. ISBN: 0-9698762-3-8

Sarah Dyck, ed./tr., *The Silence Echoes: Memoirs of Trauma & Tears* (Kitchener: Pandora Press, 1997; co-published with Herald Press). Softcover, xii, 236pp., 2 maps. ISBN: 0-9698762-7-0

Wes Harrison, *Andreas Ehrenpreis and Hutterite Faith and Practice* (Kitchener: Pandora Press, 1997; co-published with Herald Press). Softcover, xxiv, 274pp., 2 maps, index. ISBN 0-9698762-6-2

C. Arnold Snyder, *Anabaptist History and Theology: Revised Student Edition* (Kitchener: Pandora Press, 1997; co-pub. Herald Press). Softcover, xiv, 466pp., 7 maps, 28 illustrations, index, bibliography. ISBN 0-9698762-5-4

Nancey Murphy, *Reconciling Theology and Science: A Radical Reformation Perspective* (Kitchener, Ont.: Pandora Press, 1997; co-pub. Herald Press). Softcover, x, 103pp., index. ISBN 0-9698762-4-6

C. Arnold Snyder and Linda A. Huebert Hecht, eds, *Profiles of Anabaptist Women: Sixteenth Century Reforming Pioneers* (Waterloo, Ont.: Wilfrid Laurier University Press, 1996). Softcover, xxii, 442pp. ISBN: 0-88920-277-X

The Limits of Perfection: A Conversation with J. Lawrence Burkholder 2nd ed., with a new epilogue by J. Lawrence Burkholder, Rodney Sawatsky and Scott Holland, eds. (Kitchener: Pandora Press, 1996). Softcover, x, 154pp. ISBN 0-9698762-2-X

C. Arnold Snyder, *Anabaptist History and Theology: An Introduction* (Kitchener: Pandora Press, 1995). ISBN 0-9698762-0-3 Softcover, x, 434pp., 6 maps, 29 illustrations, index, bibliography.

Pandora Press
33 Kent Avenue Kitchener, ON N2G 3R2
Tel.: (519) 578-2381 / Fax: (519) 578-1826
E-mail: info@pandorapress.com
Web site: www.pandorapress.com